Victorian Policing

Gaynor Haliday

PEN & SWORD
HISTORY

First published in Great Britain in 2017 by
PEN AND SWORD HISTORY
an imprint of
Pen and Sword Books Ltd
47 Church Street
Barnsley
South Yorkshire S70 2AS

ISBN 978 1 52670 612 6

Printed and bound in England
by CPI Group (UK) Ltd, Croydon, CR0 4YY

Typeset in Times New Roman by
CHIC GRAPHICS

Pen & Sword Books Ltd incorporates the imprints of Pen & Sword
Archaeology, Atlas, Aviation, Battleground, Discovery,
Family History, History, Maritime, Military, Naval, Politics, Railways,
Select, Social History, Transport, True Crime, Claymore Press,
Frontline Books, Leo Cooper, Praetorian Press, Remember When,
Seaforth Publishing and Wharncliffe.

For a complete list of Pen and Sword titles please contact
Pen and Sword Books Limited
47 Church Street, Barnsley, South Yorkshire, S70 2AS, England
E-mail: enquiries@pen-and-sword.co.uk
Website: www.pen-and-sword.co.uk

Contents

Foreword

My interest in Victorian policing started when researching my great-great-grandfather, Thomas Bottomley, who had served in Bradford Borough Police Force in the nineteenth century.

PC Thomas Bottomley was one of fifty-eight Bradford street characters whose portraits were painted by professional watercolour artist John Sowden in the 1880s and 1890s. These included colourful personalities, such as 'Old Betty', 'Salt Jim', 'Pot Mary', 'Fish David' and 'Cheap John', who made their livings as street musicians, or by hawking and peddling all sorts of merchandise as fruit, fish or flower vendors, and were very visible on the Victorian streets. Although the portraits included blind and crippled beggars, only those who were respectable were invited to sit for Sowden at his studio.

Why my great-great-grandfather was among these individuals is somewhat a mystery. Sowden made scant diary notes about his sitters, and his notes on Thomas Bottomley in 1889 merely tell of his quiet, sensitive policing, and rumour that he never had a case reach the courts in thirty years.

Finding Thomas's records and learning that he had left his work as a woolcomber to join the police in February 1852, been superannuated in April 1891, and only once been reprimanded yet never progressed beyond the rank of constable, made me keen to discover more.

Many of the Manningham streets where he walked his beat still exist. Two of his former homes also stand. The ornate police station, once his base, remains – though in a state of disrepair. With these visible reminders of his life it was easy to conjure up a picture of him, a well-respected peace-keeper, calmly walking about on paved and well-lit streets, sending the odd drunk home to his wife and bairns, and, seeing all was in order, going home to his large family for tea.

Of course, as I discovered, nothing could be further from the truth. Contemporary newspaper accounts revealed PC Thomas Bottomley made many arrests, encountered violent criminals, and was frequently assaulted in the dark and grimy Bradford streets. But despite these tribulations he remained a local beat constable for thirty-nine years – an astonishing length of service considering how many others resigned or were dismissed after a very short period. Perhaps that is what earned him a place in the Bradford street characters' history, and grudging respect from the criminal fraternity who nick-named him 'Old Bott'.

Victorian Policing explores the lives of the courageous pioneers of policing, who worked long hours with little resource, without the assistance of later developments in technology, and with few rest days.

Coming from a wide range of backgrounds, they had little education or training to handle the roles demanded of them, yet many of the crimes and human issues they dealt with, and the hostility they encountered in doing so, were not dissimilar to those experienced by today's police forces.

The newspaper accounts of the time carried myriad reports of police activities – some amusing, some heroic, some tragic. I have tried to include pertinent examples to illustrate what working life was really like for the nineteenth-century 'bobby on the beat'.

I would particularly like to thank the following for their assistance in my research: Staff at West Yorkshire Archive Service (WYAS) for extracting the huge watch committee tomes and other records from the archives. Duncan Broady, Curator, Greater Manchester Police Museum and Archives for his help in their archives, allowing me to photograph accoutrements and documents, and for bringing items to my attention that I would otherwise never have known about. Lisa Marks, Corporate Communications Branch, Greater Manchester Police, for providing many images. Dr Martin Baines QPM and Margaret Gray, of Bradford Police Museum, for assistance and image of PC Bottomley. Pete Simpson, Cambridgeshire Police Museum for images. Holly Wells, Kent Police History Museum for images. Ross Mather, The British Police Helmet website creator, and former curator of the South Wales Police Museum.

Chapter 1

Laying the foundations

We sometimes imagine our ancestors living tough but peaceable lives – working hard in the fields, the worst disturbances being a few petty squabbles. A bucolic way of life where a police force was not required. But human nature has occasionally led some people to covet what others have – property, land, belongings, spouses – and for that reason policing in one form or another has always been necessary to try to keep the peace, deter the criminal fraternity and bring those who disobey the law to justice.

The concept of formal policing was introduced as early as 1285, when the Statute of Winchester instituted a system of watch and ward, putting in place a structure of watchmen, specifying the number of men, according to a town's population, who were to keep watch from dusk to dawn. Their key duty was to arrest any passing strangers, hold them until morning and deliver suspicious characters to the sheriff to be dealt with. These watchmen were obliged to raise the hue and cry and pursue from town to town any stranger who resisted arrest until he was caught. All able-bodied men were to assist in the chase.

Apart from this, it was up to local residents to maintain a modicum of law and order. Under the statute every man between the ages of 15 and 60 was commanded to house equipment to keep the peace, according to the quantity of land and goods he possessed.

The richest were expected to keep a horse, lance, knife, iron helmet and a long coat of chain mail known as a hauberk, while the poorest carried just bows and arrows. Each man's armoury was inspected twice a year by two high constables appointed for each hundred (a division of a county for military and judicial purposes). These high constables

1

reported any defaults of the equipment or of the watchmen, as well as reporting those in country towns who lodged strangers, and any faults in the highway, to the assigned justices, who in turn reported the matter to the king.

Further to this, the Justices of the Peace Act in 1361 instilled the principle of a working partnership between justices and constables and, by appointing people to prosecute felonies and trespasses, established statutory powers for justices of the peace.

Later, parishes and townships each elected one or more unpaid parish constables annually, compulsory appointments often unpopular with the incumbents. Usually already following a trade or occupation, the parish constables' roles included numerous and diverse functions such as collecting county and parish rates, finding transport for military forces, swearing the stocks were in good order and ready for use, and that people regularly attended church. Although their primary duty was to preserve the peace, parish constables had little or no value in crime prevention beyond that of any other able-bodied man, aside from their (often ornately decorated) staff of office. This staff was the only symbol of authority and a useful weapon of self-defence where necessary. The constables were, however, regarded as crown officers, having been required to take an oath of service to the crown on appointment.

This method of policing changed little over the centuries and a similar system was still in place in the late eighteenth and early nineteenth centuries.

As towns grew in population and prosperity, some authorities implemented a Local Improvement Act to establish more formal policing arrangements.

Each town's commissioners were entrusted with managing that town's affairs, each body aiming to address the specific needs of its local inhabitants. By petitioning Parliament, local commissioners could gain the power to levy rates, which funded highway works, lighting and sewerage schemes and a few paid police.

Birkenhead, against violent opposition to its application, received

Royal Assent for a local act in June 1833. Its commissioners, now empowered to raise £8,000 (£888,000) through rates and tolls, as well as paving, lighting and cleansing the public streets, used the money to erect a market and establish a small separate police force.

Under the command of the Captain of the Night Watch, it employed three night watchmen plus a parish constable in charge of the lock-up. Dressed in a cape and a glazed hat and carrying a lantern, these watchmen toured the streets from 9pm until 6am armed only with a staff and a stick.

A few years earlier in 1825, with a population of about 20,000 – around six times that of Birkenhead – Rochdale's police commissioners appointed thirteen men to patrol its streets at night, twelve as night watchmen and one as their captain.

In contrast, police commissioners in nearby Oldham appointed one constable in 1829, mainly responsible for rate collection and inspection of nuisances. Out of his £200 annual salary (£22,200), he had to pay the wages of two assistants known as beadles.

Although in London the ratio of police to population was higher, with around 450 constables and 4,500 night watchmen to keep the peace of almost a million-and-a-half people, that the men belonged to different (and unco-operative) organisations weakened what little power they had.

One issue common to all forces was the ineffectiveness of the night watchmen. The low pay probably only attracted those past hard work – the aged and infirm. Most were of little use for much other than lighting lamps and calling out the hours during the night.

Nodding off in their boxes at night, they were often a target for local youths who, for devilment, frequently overturned their boxes and ran off with their lanterns, leaving them stranded and unable to arrest anybody.

Although some people may have been kinder to the watchmen, perhaps slipping them a drop of rum to help them through the night, most regarded them with contempt, believing them to be corrupt and drunkards.

*

3

With the Industrial Revolution gathering pace, the rapid influx of workers into urban areas created more problems for the towns' policing arrangements. Large gangs of labouring men, brought in to build railways, factories, warehouses, mills and housing, were corralled together in lodging houses. Naturally those who lodged, adrift from their families, needed entertainment at night, and this was generally in the form of drink and women. Pubs and beerhouses thrived in the manufacturing towns. In 1824, Warrington, with fewer than 15,000 residents, had eighty-one public houses within its town centre. Drunken brawls became the norm. Industrialists were unable to control large, unruly workforces, and it appeared lawlessness ruled in the expanding towns and cities.

Urban areas were not the only places experiencing a rapid deterioration in public behaviour. Frequent stock and produce fairs in country towns drew followers who robbed and pilfered, and large numbers of people on the move in search of work attracted criminal activity.

Poaching had long been a rural problem, but ease of travel on the new canals and railways changed it from being a crime carried out by a few local men into an organised major operation, with large gangs running vicious battles with gamekeepers. Rudimentary police forces struggled with the numbers.

In 1828, even though police in Cheshire managed to arrest a gang of fifteen poachers, two companies of infantry had to be called upon to provide a safe escort when a mob of hundreds of navvies made efforts to rescue the poachers as they were being transported to court at Chester Castle.

When mob disorders such as this descended into riots, leaving magistrates no alternative other than to summon military aid, it became ever clearer that the local and varied forms of policing were pretty ineffectual against the alarmingly rapid rise in crime.

A House of Commons committee investigating the problems of policing London in 1818, after a disturbing increase in the level of crime in London since the end of the Napoleonic Wars, concluded that something should be done, but uncertain whether a police force would be acceptable in a free country did little.

On his appointment as home secretary in 1822, Robert Peel, seeing this increase in crime as a threat to society's stability, sought to establish a professionally organised, full-time police force under his control.

Progress was slow, but in 1828, after a further Commons inquiry, which reported in favour of a London police force, a bill was drafted. On 19 June 1829, Parliament finally approved Peel's Metropolitan Police Bill.

It spelled out the need for a 'more efficient System of Police in lieu of such Establishments of Nightly Watch and Nightly Police':

> *Whereas Offences against Property have of late increased in and near the Metropolis; and the local Establishments of Nightly Watch and Nightly Police have been found inadequate to the Prevention and Detection of Crime, by reason of the frequent Unfitness of the individuals employed, the Insufficiency of their Number, the limited Sphere of their Authority, and their Want of Connection and Cooperation with each other.*

As well as the detection and prevention of crime, it was envisaged that the visible presence of a uniformed and well-disciplined body of police would help to keep order on the capital's streets.

Meanwhile, in provincial towns and cities and the countryside, policing continued as before, with more towns introducing small numbers of paid police constables and watchmen.

Against a rising tide of crime there was still hostility to the notion of paying for patrols of police, even where the magistrates (usually against the idea) seemed as though they might consider it.

In the same year as the establishment of the Metropolitan Police, magistrates in Cheshire obtained permission to establish a constabulary force through an Act of Parliament. A new position of special high constable was introduced for each hundred, with responsibility for any number of subordinates, depending on the size of the district.

Clearly they were looking for more structure to policing and a higher calibre person to fill the role. An advert for a special high constable for the Bucklow Hundred stated:

> *The officer shall be able-bodied, of sound constitution and under the age of 40 years, of good character for honesty, sobriety, fidelity and activity, and be able to read and write.*[1]

There was opposition to the plan, though, from the Wirral justices, who deemed the only night patrols necessary were to protect wrecks off the coast, and such appointments should be paid for by Liverpool shipping merchants and underwriters. Even where evidence of lawlessness and the depraved habits of the population demonstrated the need for better policing, some magistrates believed it unnecessary to appoint anyone.

Nor were paid police appointments well received by the public. A letter to one newspaper referred to six paid constables as the 'new gendarmes forcibly quartered in the district'. The correspondent thought them 'a set of lazy vagabonds, harpies playing on the very vitals of the community', and prayed 'God defend us from all such spies and informers'.[2]

Signed petitions were another way the public could show their opposition to the police. One resentful (unpaid) parish constable collected many names on a petition. Unsurprisingly, nearly all the signatories were people who might be the subject of police control. Several had been charged or convicted of offences, one implicated in a murder. Others were publicans and beerhouse keepers.

With many areas still relying on unpaid or poorly paid constables and watchmen, and the crime rate continuing its upward trend, it was apparent the aversion to spending parish money on keeping order was hindering progress of the fight against crime.

The Lighting and Watching Act of 1833 allowed parish councils to levy a special rate to provide adequate numbers of day and night watchmen. Local people contributed to the cost of local policing, and that the Act was adopted in many places shows residents' concerns about the problems they encountered were so great, they were prepared to pay to solve them.

Of course, there was criticism of the way money was spent. Bradford, who had established a Watching, Lighting and Improvement Act thirty years earlier, levied a further specific rate for lighting and watching.

Perhaps more concerned with the state of the streets than crime levels, one ratepayer called attention to the neglect of the commissioners under the Lighting and Watching Act in a letter to the editor of the *Bradford Observer* on 9 April 1834. The correspondent cited several nuisances not properly addressed by the 'handsomely paid officer' responsible for such matters. He was particularly aggrieved by the filthy streets, the wool bales allowed to stand outside warehouses and the number of carts and vehicles standing in crowded thoroughfares for hours on end 'whilst their drivers caroused at public houses'.

Another correspondent (possibly the same 'ratepayer') in June of the same year complained about the flow of water in the brook running through Bradford being severely impeded by vast quantities of rubbish thrown into it and by waterwheels placed in it to obtain power. The stream was stagnant where it should have been most rapid and there was an easy solution to the problem if the surveyor (who he presumed to exist because there was a salary) would see to it that debris be cleared and the practice of throwing rubbish into the stream become a punishable offence.

In December 1834, the newspaper carried a report that a very strong muster of commissioners under Bradford's Lighting and Watching Act had held a meeting to elect a successor to the 'aged and increasingly infirm clerk'.

In recognition of his thirty-one years' long service, the commissioners voted to award him 30 shillings (£166.50) before his successor (possibly a relative) 'came handsomely forward' to propose an annuity of 51 shillings (£283), which was received by the commissioners with unanimous applause.

A new post was created – collector and deputy treasurer – to collect rates, pay wages and bills, keep accounts and mark-up the rate books. An allowance of four percent of monies collected would be paid to the incumbent, a practised and honest accountant named Thomas Haigh.

Mr William Bakes became the new surveyor with the duty of seeing the watchmen on and off every day, superintending the scavengers, and detecting all nuisances and obstructions from carts, wheelbarrows, and such, at the weekly salary of 1 guinea (£116.50).

With fifty-eight commissioners and new appointments in place, the committee congratulated itself on the fair prospect of a faithful and vigilant discharge of their duties – and hoped to be spared 'the unpleasant duty of further reproof'.

To further emphasise to ratepayers that they were doing their job, Bradford's commissioners published the following announcement:

Watching and Lighting Act

The Commissioners under this Act are empowered from time to time to appoint such a number of Watchmen to be employed within the Limits of the Act for so long a time in the Night, under such Regulation and for such wages as they (the commissioners) shall think proper, and if any Watchman appointed as aforesaid should refuse or neglect to perform his Duty, or shall in anywise misbehave himself in Execution of his Office, he shall forfeit and pay any sum not exceeding 20 shillings for every such offence.

The Watchmen are bound during the time of their being on Duty, to use their utmost endeavours to prevent any Mischief by Fire, and also any Burglaries, Robberies, Affrays or other Outrages and Disorders within the limits of the Act; and they are also required while on Duty to apprehend and secure all Malefactors, Rogues, Nightwalkers, Vagabonds and Disorderly persons, within the Limits of the Act, who shall disturb the Public Peace or whom they shall have cause to suspect of any evil Design, and to secure and keep safe custody in the Common Prison of the said Town of Bradford, or other places to be provided by the Commissioners, every such person, in order he, or she, may be conveyed as soon as conveniently may be, before some Justice of the Peace for the West Riding of the County of York, to be examined and dealt with according to Law.

The Watchmen are also bound to attend to and obey the Orders and Regulations of the Commissioners and the Directions of their Surveyor for the time being.

Any Person or Persons who shall assault, or resist, or shall promote, or encourage, the assaulting or resisting, any of the Watchmen in the Execution of their Duty shall for every such Offence, forfeit and pay any sum not exceeding Five Pounds nor less than Ten Shillings.

Any Victualler, or keeper of any Public House, who shall knowingly harbour, or entertain, any Watchman to be employed within the Limits of the Act, or permit, or suffer any such Watchman to be and remain in his House during any part of the time appointed for his being on Duty shall for every such Offence, forfeit and pay any sum not exceeding Twenty Shillings.[3]

Chapter 2

Acts and actions

After the Reform Act of 1832 had increased the electorate from around 366,000 to 650,000, albeit still only around eighteen percent of the adult male population and none of the female, constitutional reform continued with the passing of the Municipal Corporations Act in 1835.

An investigation into the state of municipal corporations found nepotism flourishing in over 180 of the 285 towns that had previously received a royal charter to have their own council or corporation. As only members of those corporations were allowed to vote, they re-elected themselves or brought friends and relatives onto the council. Thus, any rare vacancies that occurred were not filled by the best qualified candidates. Contracts for town improvements were also often awarded to corporation members or friends and not adequately supervised, resulting in overspending.

Some corporations were run on political party-lines and magistrates appointed on those same party-lines were frequently incompetent and lacked the respect of the townsfolk. And although the corporations fixed local bye-laws, policing often came under the control of a separate body of commissioners with different aspirations.

The report concluded that thorough reform was necessary to make the municipal corporations the useful and efficient instruments of local government they were supposed to be.

The Municipal Corporations Bill was voted through the House of Commons in June 1835, but almost thrown out by the House of Lords when Tory peers claimed it an attack on privileges and property. Amendments were made and Sir Robert Peel and the Duke of

Wellington ensured the antagonists were prevented from throwing out the Bill. It became law in September 1835.

The Act abolished the closed corporations. New rules stated that borough councils were to be elected by all male ratepayers who had been resident in that town for three years. Councillors were elected for a three-year term, although a third retired annually. These councillors would elect a mayor to serve for a year, and a group of aldermen to serve for six years. To ensure accounts were now properly audited, a paid town clerk and treasurer would be appointed.

One hundred and seventy-eight boroughs were reformed under this Act. Those hundred-or-so remaining unreformed either fell into disuse or were later replaced.

Towns and cities without a council could apply for incorporation if they so wished. The complicated and potentially expensive procedure meant many towns failed to apply. However, industrial towns such as Birmingham and Manchester quickly seized the initiative and became boroughs in 1838.

Although it established the principle of town councils being accountable, the Act had some failings.

In not compelling the councils to make social improvements to ensure the drains were effective and the streets kept clean, very few took any action to improve public health.

It also only *permitted* boroughs to form a police force, and without being forced to do so, fewer than 100 of the 178 boroughs took immediate action.

The reformed borough of Leicester (population 45,000), like many other towns, already had a police force of sorts.

One of the first undertakings of its newly appointed watch committee was to assess the present state of the existing constabulary before making any arrangements for a new system. It found the town divided into fifteen wards, each with a ward constable, with thirteen of the ward constables also having a deputy known as a head borough – plus forty-five parish constables sworn in for the borough. Above all this was a high constable paid an annual salary of £50 (£5,550). Apart from eight of the constables, who were paid £10 (£1,110) annually, none of the others received regular payment. Any monies they did receive in exercising their public duties came through fees and perquisites, arising from issuing warrants, granting summonses, special attendance at fairs, markets, and sessions, carrying maces, waiting feasts, and from chance cases of assault and street brawls.

This flawed mode of paying men engaged in arduous important work led some parish constables to generate disturbances in order to obtain or extort fees, making them unpopular and devoid of any moral influence on the population.

As well as the unpaid constables, there were six watchmen and two other constables, paid for by various private subscriptions in particular neighbourhoods.

This miscellany of constables and watchmen was woefully inadequate. The watch committee found many of the men unfit for duty and 'otherwise objectionable'.

It was resolved for a new arrangement to supersede all. It would be one uniform system emanating from one centre and encompassing the whole town.

Setting up a new professional police force was an onerous task. Recruiting and equipping a body of paid men had cost implications and councils could now be held to account by the ratepayers if they considered the mission poorly executed.

Like many boroughs that were early adopters, Leicester looked to the Metropolitan Police for guidance, instructing the town clerk to write to Colonel Rowan, the founding senior commissioner of the Metropolitan Police, asking for a copy of their rules and an active and intelligent police officer to be sent.

When the reply from London was to regret they could not attend to Leicester's request immediately, as there had been so many similar applications from other towns, a deputation from the finance committee travelled to London to present a renewed application. The plea worked and within a few days the secretary of state's office advised police officer Frederick Goodyer was on his way.

In the meantime, the council and watch committee met to examine how the heavy, but unavoidable, expense of a well-organised police force for the borough might be funded.

From whatever rates previously levied for local government, only £130 (£14,430) had been expended directly on the police, therefore it was clear this amount would need to be supplemented. The watch committee ventured to suggest the council might liquidate some of the corporation's assets by selling off building land and tithes belonging to it, placing the monies raised into a separate fund. This would help to cover the expense of establishing a police force without having to tax the town's inhabitants. All concurred.

It was agreed to serve notice on each officer and member of the former corporation, calling on him to return whatever corporation monies he might have in his possession (thought to be considerable sums) or to state to whom he may recently have handed over any such property. Refusal to do so would result in legal action.

The watch committee, updating the council on its progress in establishing the police force, stated its intention to organise an effective a police force as possible (with all due regard to economy) as soon as the experienced officer from the Metropolitan Police arrived. The committee, although independent of the council, also agreed not to adopt any police plan without the council's sanction, and until the force was fully operational could not determine any future cost to Leicester's ratepayers, though estimated it would be between 6d and 1 shilling in the pound per year (£2.77 – £5.55).

Ahead of Mr Goodyer's arrival on 13 January, the town clerk placed an advertisement for constables in the local paper:

> *All Persons desirous of the situation of CONSTABLE under the Watch Committee appointed by the Town Council are requested to apply the Town Hall, Thursday next, the 14th instant at ten o'clock in the morning. They must be able to write, and will be required to produce written testimonials as to fitness and character. No-one need apply who is below five feet seven inches in stature,*

or under 23 or above 40 years of age. Residents will be preferred. (Leicester Chronicle, 9 January 1836.)

To avoid the appearance of favouritism, all were given equal and open chance of applying, but the intention was to select only men of character and intelligence from the anticipated large number of applicants.

Despite the stipulations of 'those who need not apply', some candidates were too short in stature, others too feeble or too old. Some were deemed objectionable characters or rejected for other reasons. Those who could not write were also turned away. After all applicants had been seen, the number of approved men was insufficient so a further advertisement was placed, and within a week there were enough suitable and efficient men from which to form a police force.

But what should they pay the men, and how many constables did they actually need?

Juggling issues of cost with the need to recruit and retain men with the 'happy combination of intelligence, character, physical strength and courage' to carry out the arduous and unremitting duties, protecting life and property both day and night, the watch committee decided a salary of 18 shillings a week (£99.90) – not much above the average paid to better classes of workmen – would secure intelligent and respectable men to work as common constables. And following the example of the London police, sergeants would receive 6d per day (£2.77) more than constables.

In terms of the number of men, the watch committee had originally proposed forty would be sufficient, but later stated its members 'after mature and repeated consideration and having made the circuit of the town, and well considered its dimensions, are unanimously of opinion that the most certain and effectual protection of the town by night as well as by day, would be better served by having a police force of 50 men'. (*Leicester Chronicle*, 23 January 1836)

The committee was concerned that if there were insufficient men to quell street brawls, and if burglaries and robberies were as frequent under the new system as the old, then justifiably there would be complaints and dissatisfaction among the borough's inhabitants.

After much debate the council agreed economy should be secondary, and efficiency a primary consideration in organising the new police. Therefore, fifty was probably a better number.

To take control of the new force, the watch committee appointed Mr Goodyer as inspector at £100 (£11,100) per year. As well as the excellent testimonial he had brought with him, the committee considered when introducing a new system it was indispensable to have a person thoroughly acquainted with it to initiate the men. Beyond this lay the conviction that 'an intelligent stranger, free from any local bias or feeling, would have more admitted and allowed moral influence than any townsman, however well-respected' (*Leicester Chronicle*, 23 January 1836).

In search of a suitable police station the watch committee, with Mr Goodyer, having visited and inspected the existing station-houses, the engine-house and lower part of the Exchange, suggested the room adjoining their meeting room in the Guildhall be most appropriate. As a store for the previous corporation's crockery and dishes, it no longer served any useful or important purpose. The outbuildings, previously used as kitchens, were also redundant and could be appropriated to keep the fire engines under the control and protection of the police. Another advantage of the location was its situation in a quiet private street.

The inhabitants of Leicester were informed their new police force would commence duty on 11 February 1836 by notices displayed in the town hall and church, which detailed the division of day and night shifts.

The day duty was split into four periods of four hours and two teams of five constables would cover these, while a sergeant and constable remained in the station house. Night duty was a straight eight hours on the streets for two sergeants and thirty-two constables, again leaving two men in the station house. One sergeant and two constables would be off-duty, on call for emergencies, and this would be taken in rotation.

Dressed in top hat and blue tail-coats, armed with a staff and carrying a rattle to summon assistance the new constables were sworn in on 10 February, promising to serve the king and 'behave themselves according to the best of their skill and judgement'.[4]

Training was through copies of the printed instruction book, adapted from the Metropolitan Police's rule book – omitting some rules and introducing others – to tailor them to Leicester's specific requirements. Each constable was issued with his own copy to digest and thoroughly understand. In addition, there were many laws to learn.

Although three months after its formation the town council and watch committee were congratulating each other on the success of the new police force, others in the town were not so complimentary.

Letters to the *Leicester Journal* complaining that as the £3,000 (£333,000) expense of the police force was now to be 'wrung from the pockets of the ratepayers' (the sale of assets having not yet been approved), suggested it would be better to reduce force numbers, especially during the day. This illusion of an overmanned police force stemmed from the sight of officers, who having been on night duty and refreshed themselves with sleep for a portion of the day, spent the remainder of their off-duty period walking about the streets in uniform – it being requisite for uniform to be worn at all times.

Although consideration and approval was given to reducing the number of men to forty as vacancies occurred, it is unclear whether this went ahead. A reduction in the rate of pay was also discussed, but it was agreed the salary was well-earned. At least one constable had already left the force for employment at only half his policeman's pay because he found the duty too fatiguing. With assaults on the police commonplace, the work could be painful – as many as 116 charges being brought in the first ten months. One constable told of being so ill-used when trying to arrest a vagrant brandishing a poker, he'd had to go to bed, but was in so much pain he could not turn in it.

The ratepayers of Leicester were not the only ones to grumble about their police force. It was reported in a council meeting – to much laughter – that the people of neighbouring Loughborough were also complaining about the Leicester police, because in consequence of the force's efficiency, the vagrants who once flocked to Leicester were now favouring Loughborough with their company.

As other reformed boroughs began to organise police forces, it was clear each had its own idea of the best structure for its own town, meaning numbers, structure, pay rates and equipment varied.

Boroughs with ports seem to have been early adopters. Dover, Folkestone, Hull, Ipswich, Liverpool, Portsmouth, Plymouth and Southampton each started a police force within months of the Act being passed.

Plymouth's (population 34,000) watch committee held its first meeting on 16 January 1836, recruiting unpaid householders who were already operating under the old watch and ward system for paid daytime duties. It divided the borough into six wards and appointed one man in each ward to be ward constable. Their names and places of residence were published and posted on public buildings around town.

An inspector was appointed at 18 shillings a week (£99.90) and six 'street-keepers' all receiving 15 shillings (£83.25) per week. They were allocated to the wards and expected to be constantly on duty during the day. A superintendent at a salary of £40 a year (£4,440) was placed in charge of the night police, which consisted of four captains, six rounders, ten patrolmen and fifty-four watchmen of the night. This new police force commenced duties on Saturday 26 March 1836.

However, within six months, after some deliberation as to its effectiveness, Plymouth's force was reorganised to consist of a superintendent at £65 per year (£7,215), three inspectors each paid 18 shillings a week (£99.90) and twenty-seven constables at 15 shillings a week each (£83.25), eventually commencing its work at the end of October.

Ipswich's (population 23,000) fledgling police force established on 1 March 1836 had three inspectors each paid £1 a week (£111) to overlook and superintend a total of fifteen constables, all paid 14 shillings a week (£77.70) and divided into three teams, one that worked during the day, the other two at night.

Their uniform was a beaver skin top hat, blue swallowtail coat and

17

trousers – white for summer and blue for winter. Each man carried a staff and wore a red and white armband issued at the start of every tour of duty to indicate an officer was on duty.

The new constables in Ipswich soon adopted the habits of their night watchmen predecessors, and within nine months, nine of the fifteen had been disciplined for offences relating to drunkenness.

As new boroughs were created, so too were their police forces. Nothing was achieved without debate and disagreement, but when in October 1838 Manchester and five other townships (Chorlton upon Medlock, Hulme, Ardwick, Beswick and Cheetham) merged to create the Borough of Manchester, it encountered more issues than most.

Some of the townships objected to the legality of incorporation and in many cases continued to operate side-by-side. The coroners were particularly opposed to the situation, and several inquests were held twice, once by the borough coroner and once by the township coroner.

Nonetheless, a watch committee was formed on 23 January 1839 to oversee the establishment of a professional borough police force. With a total population of around 230,000 spread over a wide area, and each township having previously maintained separate policing arrangements, there was much to consider.

By 25 March, a detailed structure for the new force was in place, led by a head constable at a salary of £400 per year (£44,400). Beneath him was an indoor superintendent at £250 per year (£27,750), four other superintendents all at £150 a year (£16,650), twenty inspectors, all paid 27 shillings a week each (£150), eight indoor constables at 25 shillings a week (£139) each, and 295 constables, every one paid 17 shillings a week (£94.35). There were also seven lock-up keepers and seven clerks. The annual wages bill would be around £17,000 (£1,887,000), plus a uniforms cost of £1,700 (£188,700), and £1,025 for other expenses (£114,000).

Five candidates were interviewed for the post of head constable, Richard Beswick being appointed on 3 June 1839, and in the following few weeks many men previously employed in the townships were appointed as constables and other ranks.

The well-documented watch committee proceedings reveal additional appointments, purchases of accoutrements to clothe and equip the men, disciplinary actions and other considerations similar to those of any other borough, until almost the end of September. However, all was not well in the new Borough of Manchester.

In August 1839, barely six weeks since the formation of the new police force, the *Manchester Courier and Lancashire General Advertiser* published a statement that as well as the incorporation of the townships into a borough, the police rate being imposed to cover the cost of the force was also deemed illegal. Ninety-one of the police commissioners agreed. In consequence, the people of Manchester refused to pay their rates and only 0.6% of the total borough rate of £41,000 (£4,551,000) was collected.

The dispute questioned whether the rate should be that stipulated in the Metropolitan Police Act or one provided for in the local act, although there was a clause in the Metropolitan Police Act (applicable to Manchester), which provided that all rates levied before the passing of that Act should continue to be collected as before.

Despite a motion being carried stating the allegations made regarding the rate being illegal had no grounds, a Bill 'for improving the police in Manchester, adopting the Metropolitan Police Act as a basis for raising a rate to defray the expense of the police' was put before Parliament.

In early October 1839, Colonel Sir Charles Shaw was appointed chief commissioner of the Manchester New Police, tasked with putting into force this new Act of Parliament by 17 October. His first duty was to examine all men so recently recruited to the force, as the introduction of the Act effectively put an end to their employment. Aiming to retain every man – providing his conduct, character and physical ability warranted it – he sought testimonials and opinions and considered each man's previous service, but was wise enough to admit he might make mistakes or be misinformed (and therefore not all men might be as satisfactory as he hoped). In such cases he believed the situation would be speedily detected and remedied.

However, despite his aims, Charles Shaw did not immediately appoint everyone who had been previously employed.

Seventy-three constables were placed on a reserve list to fill vacancies as and when they occurred (fairly frequently), but another twenty-five were found by the police surgeon to be unfit for duty, while a further fifteen failed to attend the required medical examination and were therefore inadmissible to the force.

The head constable was burdened with summoning the unfortunate men to advise them their services would not be required after 16 October, although most would receive some payment in lieu of notice.

Four days later a letter was received by the watch committee, signed by nine inspectors 'much surprised and hurt' to find their names omitted in the appointments made by the chief commissioner, and that their services were to be dispensed with at a month's notice. Since they had been in the police service for nearly six years, they had great concerns about 'obtaining situations in any other pursuits'. Seemingly, other offers of police employment were subsequently made, perhaps at reduced positions, but four of the nine men declined and were denied any further financial allowance.

From the outset, Charles Shaw was subject to a great deal of criticism. In a letter to the mayor on 10 December he wrote of the 'various and vexatious difficulties which have been thrown in my way since my arrival in Manchester'. Reports of every possible nature, calculated to cause either misapprehension of his measures or to be upheld for public disapproval, had apparently been circulated.

Claiming in his letter that he had found three district police establishments with a numerical strength of around 600 men (under no general control) at a cost of £40,000 (£4,440,000), his budget being only £16,500 (£1,831,500), Sir Charles had had no option but to limit recruitment initially, selecting a proportionate number from each force to swear in just 200 constables on 17 October. He admitted it had soon become obvious this was not enough, so a further 100 men had been appointed, giving a new total of 300 constables, plus officers.

Sir Charles' claim that he had inherited a force of 600 at a cost of £40,000 seems at odds with the size and cost of the force originally recruited by the watch committee in June (the lower figure and cost being later repeated in the watch committee minutes in 1842, when it once again took charge of policing Manchester).

But using his own statistics to emphasise the increase in efficiency of the new force over its short-lived predecessor, Charles Shaw demonstrated that, although police constable numbers were halved, the number of criminals committed for trial was around the same. If it was necessary to increase the force's numbers and therefore the cost – estimated to be now £21,500 to £22,000 (£2,386,500 – £2,442,000) – he felt confident the public would be supportive when he needed to appeal to them for further funding to continue his work.

Thus buoyed by self-praise, Sir Charles continued to assert his control over matters.

His assignment continued until October 1842, when (after the Charter of Incorporation of the Borough of Manchester had been confirmed by the judges of Westminster Hall in July) the Act in force for regulating the police in Manchester under the direction of the chief commissioner was allowed to expire. The council pledged to take measures 'for the continuance of an efficient police force within the Borough, so that on the expiration of such Acts there shall be no interval without an ample and efficient police force being maintained for the maintenance of the public peace, and the preservation of good order in within the Borough'.[5]

As the Manchester police force came under the watch committee's control once again, the men in the force had to be re-appointed. With no time for any alternative course of action, the whole force of 313 was sworn in on 1 October. Within a month, fifty-three were dismissed for being ineffective.

The original head constable, Richard Beswick, who had served well under Charles Shaw, was appointed indoor superintendent of the borough at the annual salary of £250 (£27,750), and temporarily took control and direction of the police under the watch committee until a chief constable could be appointed to replace the chief commissioner.

21

Seventeen men applied for the chief constable's position, with the shortlist of four including Richard Beswick. The watch committee appointed Captain Edward Willis, deputy chief constable of Lancashire Police, his salary of £450 per year (£49,950) being £250 less than that paid to Shaw. Beswick was appointed to the new role of chief superintendent of police at a salary of £350 (£38,850) per year, and the newspapers reported he might use his considerable skills to develop and improve the force's detective department.

While urban areas started to bring law and order to their streets, the preservation of peace and protection of inhabitants in the countryside was still the responsibility of the reluctant parish constable.

A royal commission appointed in 1836 revealed its findings in the Constabulary Forces Report in March 1839. The three Constabulary commissioners included Sir Charles Rowan, commissioner of the Metropolitan Police.

The report made grim reading.

Of the estimated 11,000 to 20,000 people in gaol, more than half of them were habitual criminals, with those in rural districts having been at large and living by depredation for over five years. That this was twice the length of time that prisoners in towns had lived by dishonest means was attributed to the lack of a trained force in rural areas and that unpaid constables possessed no information about habitual thieves.

Crime was also rising in rural areas. Paid forces instituted in municipal towns had rendered considerable benefits to the towns' inhabitants, not necessarily by preventing or suppressing all evil, but by shifting a portion of it into the adjacent countryside. A large proportion of prisoners in the county gaols were people who had migrated from towns.

One example of the industrial problems manifesting themselves on the quiet countryside was in 1839, when 2,000 labourers building the railway line between Chester and Birkenhead went on strike over wages. Armed with picks and other implements, they rampaged through the countryside, robbing and pillaging travellers and inhabitants, and taking possession of an entire village. The newly formed Chartist movement posed similar threats and concerns of riotous behaviour.

Farmers experienced large-scale thefts of agricultural produce from their fields and were fearful of travelling home alone in the dark from markets, since miles of highway were without adequate constabulary protection, allowing robbery and violence to prevail.

Where there had been trials of paid and well-appointed constabulary forces in rural districts, the commissioners found these districts had been kept free from 'vagrants, mendicants and migratory depredators'. This had resulted in a reduction in thefts of produce and crimes against property.

In addition, 'disorders in beer-shops and ill-regulated houses of public resort and other sources of temptation and causes of domestic distress and immorality' had been repressed.

Even the habitual misdemeanours of the resident delinquents had been prevented; some having reformed, others now constrained to courses of honest industry.

Little wonder the commission recommended the establishment of a paid constabulary force, trained, appointed and organised on the same principles as the Metropolitan Police, as a 'primary remedy for the evils set forth'.

The County Police Act 1839 (also known as the Rural Police Act or Rural Constabularies Act), like the Municipal Corporations Act, only *permitted* any of the fifty-four counties in England and Wales to raise and equip a paid police force.

Instead of a watch committee, county constabularies were overseen by justices of the peace in general or quarter sessions – a county being defined as 'any County, Riding or Division having a separate Court of Quarter Sessions of the Peace or in which separate County Rates are made'.

Those adopting the Act appointed a chief constable and no more than one paid police officer for every thousand inhabitants. Where counties were small, one chief constable could be appointed to two or more neighbouring counties.

Pay scales were similar to those of police in urban areas, but represented double the pay of local agricultural workers.

Boroughs within counties that had already established professional police forces continued to maintain a separate force. Those that had not, faced pressure from the county constabularies to allow the borough's policing to fall under their control.

Wiltshire was the first county to form a constabulary, with the Court of Quarter Sessions agreeing to adopt the Act on 13 November 1839. On 5 December, its magistrates approved the appointment of former naval commander Samuel Meredith as chief constable.

Amendments to the Act were made in 1840, which included permitting the levy of a special police rate to finance a constabulary, and allowing justices to acquire land and buildings and borrow money to create police stations and cells for the temporary custody of prisoners.

Boroughs could consolidate their forces with that of the surrounding county, and justices were empowered to divide counties into districts with a population of not less than 25,000 inhabitants.

The justices were also allowed to disband the constabulary, giving six months' notice to the home secretary, if in their opinion the force was no longer needed.

Yet another policing Act was introduced in 1842 to 'infuse new life into the decrepit parochial system', where counties resisted implementing the 1839 Act.

The Parochial Constables Act and an amendment (the Superintending Constables Act) allowed magistrates to build district lock-ups and recruit paid (and hopefully more professional) full-time superintending constables to preside over the district and the parish constables within it. The parish constables would continue to be paid through the scale of allowances for various duties. It seemed a less costly option than a county constabulary, but in effect savings were probably little, as other bodies were paid to carry out some of the work that generally fell under the remit of a county constabulary. Still relying heavily on the parish constables, policing of this sort was likely to remain inadequate.

However, one zealous magistrate saw the introduction of this Act as a chance to disband the Worcestershire constabulary, asserting that ratepayers should now avail themselves of the power of self-government given to them. He claimed the force's benefit had not been equal to its expense and sought a resolution to remove the constabulary as from the Easter Sessions of 1844.

He argued that all they received from the county force were quarterly reports – not worth the paper on which they were written – daily returns containing many instances of a most trifling nature, and some apprehensions, perhaps, illegal. Much of this was down to the inefficiency of the chief constable, he claimed, also contending that the chief constable, by his issuing of constables' instruction books, caused the constables to acknowledge his authority, when in fact it was the magistrates who should be in charge.

It was counter-argued that, among other issues, the new force had amply demonstrated its effectiveness in reducing crime and bringing orderliness to the county. By way of illustration it was reported sheep thefts in 1838–39 had been seventy-six and no one had been convicted, whereas in 1840–41 there had been nineteen stolen and in 1842–43 only three, and in each of those years the perpetrators had been brought to justice.

It was moved that to revert to the old disjointed system, attended by all its former evils, would be foolish and the zealous magistrate's resolution to disband the force was soundly defeated.

As towns grew and sought incorporation as boroughs, they followed the processes and structures of those professional police forces already created, and as a result avoided some of the tribulations experienced by the pioneering boroughs.

Salford had shown initial reticence in becoming a borough, but when the recently formed Lancashire Constabulary indicated it would impose a professional police force on the town, Salford's dignitaries soon sought a charter of incorporation, preferring to keep policing matters under their own control. When it became a borough in 1844, Salford made implementation of a police force a priority.

Through the detailed inventory commissioned by Salford's watch committee, it is interesting to learn what it already had in place as a non-professional (but paid) force.

Headed by a superintendent at £200 a year (£22,200), there were four beadles for day duty plus a night superintendent, three inspectors of watchmen and eighteen watchmen for night duty. Every watchman received 15 shillings 6d in summer (£86.00), with an extra shilling (£5.55) a week in winter. Beadles, who worked longer hours, were paid proportionately more. There was also provision of three supernumeraries on standby, each at 6d a night (£2.77), to be paid by the man for whom they worked if they had to cover his duty.

Salford had already equipped these men with uniforms, greatcoats, lanterns and rattles, and held pistols, swords, leg-irons and handcuffs at the police station and the town's two lock-ups.

Since neighbouring Manchester's force, now under the efficient and highly satisfactory control of Captain Willis, was progressing apace, Salford's town clerk was asked to procure a copy of the rules and regulations adopted by Manchester, the amount of wages paid and cost of clothing.

Seeking and heeding this advice presumably made Salford's transition from township to borough far less problematic than Manchester's.

The burgeoning township of Bradford did not become a borough until April 1847, when it received a Charter of Incorporation to include within its boundaries the townships of Bowling, Horton and Manningham.

When its watch committee met on 13 November 1847, it formed a sub-committee to define the limits by which to extend the existing police force and to suggest the number of police necessary for purpose, with their respective wages. It was proposed Charles Ingham be appointed chief constable at a salary of £220 per year (£24,420), out of which he would need to pay an efficient clerk not less than £70 (£7,770).

That same day Charles Ingham, aged 40 and already a constable of the town, submitted his application for the position, with several character testimonials. He ably answered all questions put to him by the sub-committee regarding the numbers of day and night police which, in his opinion, would be necessary, and several other matters.

However, on referral back to the watch committee it was considered preferable to advertise the position more widely in Bradford, Leeds and Manchester, and in a paper known as the *Weekly Despatch for Chief Constables*.

A shortlist of five was drawn up from the twenty-nine applicants – including Charles Ingham. On 26 November, the final vote went to Mr William Leveratt, a superintendent from Liverpool. Bradford's watch committee wrote to Liverpool's watch committee requesting an early release from his duties, and by 2 December, William Leveratt was able to deliver his recommendations regarding the policing of Bradford to the sub-committee. Perhaps reluctant to share a portion of his salary with an efficient clerk, he declined to appoint one, believing any clerk's duties could be performed by himself and the night superintendent.

Recruitment began, tenders were placed for clothing and other accoutrements, rule books printed, books and documents procured and, on 1 January 1848, the Bradford Borough Constabulary Force came into being, manned and clothed but not quite fully equipped.

A detailed report of the men, their clothing and accoutrements was sent to the Rt Hon Sir George Grey, Baronet, Home Secretary, quantifying the annual cost as £3,749 (£416,139).

With various Acts in place for both urban and rural areas to levy rates, one might assume that people on councils and justices in sessions would have expedited their responsibilities to provide professional policing for their respective inhabitants. But with no obligation, petty jealousies about control, a reluctance to commit funding and alternative systems available, policing rumbled on in a disconnected manner for another decade. In the early 1850s, with only 12,000 professional policemen in England and Wales, it was still possible for criminals to carry out their nefarious deeds virtually unimpeded by the law.

Lord Palmerston, appointed home secretary in December 1852, unimpressed with the country's fragmented and rudimentary police force ordered a select committee to 'consider the expediency of adopting a more uniform system of police in England, Scotland and Wales'. The findings of the inquiry were reported in June 1853.

Having cross-examined chief constables, magistrates, solicitors, superintending constables and mayors from various counties, some of which had adopted the 1839 Act, others of which had not, it was found there were huge differences in the ratios of policemen to inhabitants, and costs and responsibilities varied too.

In addition, although there had been improvements in policing since the last commission in 1836, in counties that had not adopted the Act the situation had further deteriorated.

The select committee deemed vagrancy to be the greatest factor in the cause of crime, with one chief constable stating that, in the end, all vagrants became thieves. For many living in rural areas, vagrancy was a way of life. People took work where they could find it, and when there was none, tramped on. Well-trodden paths were visible where scores of vagrants had crossed the same fields for years.

Norfolk had established a professional police force and, although the chairman of the quarter sessions had initially questioned the policy of doing so, he had observed its progress compared with the old system and was in no doubt the county now derived advantage in every way. He told of how, on several occasions in recent times, vagrants brought before him in the court had pleaded to be let go this time as they 'did not know there was such a force', vowing they would go out of the county and into Cambridgeshire or Lincolnshire. As far as he knew they had kept their word.

It seemed they had, as with the arrival of all the rogues from Norfolk, Cambridgeshire magistrates, who had been very much opposed to adopting a constabulary, had given up their resistance.

As well as being better at dealing with crime after the event, a police presence had the effect of reducing offences since the perpetrators knew they were more likely to be detected.

One farmer and land agent from Essex told of his village's notoriety for its home-grown depredators, with at least one villager in gaol all the time. Now, he said, there was none, it being 'not worth their while to go out when there is such difficulty getting home with stolen property', knowing they were being observed.

The police were also now much more readily available to be called on for assistance if a person was spotted acting suspiciously. In the old parish system, the constable was too much part of the community and less inclined to act against his neighbours and relatives. But as one reprobate admitted, when brought up for stealing produce from the fields, 'I knew I was being watched now, when I saw the shining hat above the hedge.'

In stark contrast were the crime rates in counties that had adopted a force under the Parochial Constables Act. Even though there were now paid superintending constables, counties such as Lincolnshire and Northumberland had only a dozen or so men on horseback to patrol vast acreages of uninhabited land.

The parish constables they relied on for local assistance were at best plain inefficient, but generally lazy or ignorant. One man, now chief constable of the City of Bath police, who had previously been a superintending constable in Northumberland, had found parish constables in that county so corrupt he was obliged to have nothing to do with them and had had to act entirely alone. Many had been convicted of felony and others kept company with the most notorious thieves and poachers.

Groups of farmers and land agents created their own associations to prosecute felons for offences against property. Places like Caistor in Lincolnshire were apparently overrun with bad characters – sheep stealing and breaking into granaries and outhouses – with at least one offence per week. Even the poor were not immune from being robbed. One family had had to sit up all night to prevent the pig they had slaughtered being stolen from them.

County borders also caused issues with policing. Captain John Woodford, Lancashire Constabulary's chief constable, had problems with Yorkshire's police force.

Police in Todmorden, a town straddling the Yorkshire-Lancashire border, had insinuated that Lancashire constables were going into Yorkshire for the sole purpose of obtaining cases to bring before the magistrates. Of course, this would have taken possible fees and earnings from the Yorkshiremen still working under the parochial system. The truth was that properly trained Lancashire constables, seeing drunkenness, brawling in public houses and pugilistic fighting, crossed the invisible county border line to suppress the disorders.

However, due to complaints from Yorkshire, Captain Woodford had ordered his men to only venture over the border when in pursuit of thieves. In consequence disorders were left to continue and escalate: 'It is now the business of Yorkshire people to keep order in their own county,' he declared.

Armed with the select committee's findings and recommendations, Palmerston initially drafted a new Police Bill in 1854, but twice encountered resistance to the new legislation, partly because there was to be no financial support from government. On 4 February 1855, Palmerston was invited to become prime minister and appointed former home secretary Sir George Grey to fill the vacant role once more.

With support from Palmerston and further changes to the committee's eight original proposed reforms, Grey secured the passage of the County and Borough Police Act through Parliament on 10 March 1856. It received royal assent on 21 July.

The new Act obligated all counties and boroughs to have a police force. A quarter of the funding for wages and clothing would come from treasury grants – but only if the newly created Inspectorate of Constabulary found the force to be efficient. Each chief constable would be required to submit an annual report regarding the state of crime in his constabulary to the home secretary.

The Act only applied to England and Wales, Scotland having passed its own legislation. Nor did it include the Metropolitan Police or the City of London Police.

Smaller boroughs with populations below 20,000 would be policed by surrounding counties and the five smallest counties were each amalgamated with a larger neighbour for policing purposes.

Cheshire Constabulary, in existence through its private Act of Parliament in 1829, was to be replaced by a force under the new Act.

With around 230 separate police forces and large variations in pay and service conditions, the aim of complete uniformity of a national police force was not achieved, but instead a compromise of central management coupled with local control existed, adhering to minimum standards set out by government inspectors.

Chapter 3

Recruitment, training and progression

Most forces, whether a borough or a county force (either pre- or post-1856), had similar standards for the calibre of their new recruits. One example is the advertisement placed in the *Bradford Observer* on 9 December 1847, by James Cooper, Bradford's town clerk, which stipulated that applications for the superintendent, sergeants, day and night constables and two detective officers had to be in the applicants' own handwriting and be accompanied by testimonials as to character and fitness. Candidates had to read and write well, be of strong constitution and sound health, taller than 5 feet 7 inches and aged between 22 and 35. Unlike the parish constables of old, they would not be permitted to follow any other occupation.

In order to recruit, and importantly to retain, a stable, competent and conscientious workforce, pay scales were set to attract the more ambitious semi-skilled men – those who sought secure employment. Being a police constable was not a soft option, but offered a steady, regular income and the potential to develop a career, even for men with little formal education. At a time when a man could lose his job at a stroke, the certainty of no decline in trade and benefits such as clothing and boots should have made policing an attractive option. And providing they met the physical criteria, the opportunity was open to men from any background.

The selection process was, out of necessity, swift and fairly rigorous. In Bradford the advertisement attracted around 600 applicants – ten times more than were required. When the candidates appeared before the watch committee at 10am on 15 December 1847, their reading and writing skills were examined and personal details checked. Each underwent a physical examination – in Bradford's case this was carried out by one of the aldermen at no cost to the individual – but in most forces this was done at the applicant's own expense. In the subsequent days, testimonials were followed up and the successful men appointed on 18 December.

New constables came from a variety of backgrounds: unskilled men such as farm workers and labourers; semi-skilled men employed in the woollen or heavy manufacturing industries; craftsmen, including shoemakers and tailors; and former militia men. To maintain some continuity in the force and offer guidance to new men, many boroughs offered positions to the existing watchmen. In Bradford, they accounted for over a third of the new night police, and Manchester almost half. Birmingham, on the other hand, reported they were sorry to say that comparatively few of the old police watch were eligible for appointment to the new force.

In addition to the appointed constables, supernumeraries were engaged – fit men out of which any could be selected to replace others who were discharged, ill or absent for any other cause. By having supernumeraries ready to step in, a force could be kept at full strength. Men could apply to a chief constable to be added to the supernumerary list and their names entered into a book to be brought before the watch committee for approval.

New recruits in every force had their conditions of service clearly spelled out so 'no complaint may be hereafter made upon their being enforced'.

These included obedience, honesty and devotion to duty, and to allay the public's suspicion that police might spy on them, constables were required to appear at all times in complete police uniform. The uniform had to be well-maintained and should the constable resign or be dismissed, every piece was to be returned in good condition. Perhaps fearful a constable might abscond with his uniform if sacked, the conditions in Bradford demanded he pay a £3 deposit (£333) to the chief constable – more than three weeks wages.

Many forces recycled uniforms where possible, and Surrey's

constabulary was probably not the only force to deduct a sum 'not exceeding ten shillings' from the pay due to any police officer on his quitting the job. The money was used to pay for the uniform to be altered for his successor.

A constable could only voluntarily quit the service with permission and a month's notice without forfeiting pay, but was liable to immediate dismissal for unfitness, negligence or misconduct. His place of residence was also subject to watch committee approval.

Most men entered the force with no previous experience. New recruits were sent out in the first week either in the company of an experienced constable or with an inspector on his rounds, for on-the-job training. Where possible they attended court daily.

After this brief initiation, they were placed on their own beats, and although veteran officers were on hand to help new men with the ins and outs of the job over a long period of informal instruction, they were pretty much in at the deep end.

However, every man was issued with a rule book from which to learn which situations they were to interfere in and the legal powers they possessed when they met with resistance. The rule book asserted that, as the legitimate peace officer of his district, a police constable was invested with considerable powers through common law and Acts of Parliament. Although all ranks were urged to become perfectly acquainted with the subject so they might act effectively and safely in their protection of the public, day-to-day policing mainly fell on the constables.

Usually their duties were bounded by specific hours, but those off-duty were liable to be called upon at any time and had to be ready to work at the shortest notice. They were required to assemble at their police station in good time to commence their duties.

Many new constables found the work not to their liking. It was physically and emotionally demanding with long periods of duty patrolling the dark narrow streets, often during inclement weather, with an ever-present threat of being assaulted. Discipline was strict and constables regularly found themselves brought before the watch committee by their sergeant on what may have appeared to them as the most trifling of offences.

Constables generally reported to a sergeant who passed the orders transmitted to him from his superior to the constables before going on their beats. As he was held accountable for the security of life and property within his section and the preservation of the peace and general good order while on duty, it fell upon the sergeant to be active, vigilant and prudent and to try instil these qualities into the men under his command.

He remained on duty with the men, constantly checking them and their whereabouts, and inspecting them before and after every shift, noting their behaviour and police matters in his pocket book. Any misconduct was handled with immediacy and the constable directed to attend the next sitting of the watch committee, who would hear the charge, any defence and take a decision as to any necessary punishment.

Sergeants had little management training and the 'do as I say or I'll take you to the chief constable' approach rankled with some men, who either did not understand the consequences of neglecting their duties or were plainly obstinate.

One constable, challenged by his superior who had observed him neglecting to try every shop door in a street to check they were locked, said he would try them next time he walked round, refusing to obey the command to 'do them now'. When threatened with being taken before the chief constable, the constable retorted he would be glad to do so as he 'didn't care a bugger' for either his boss or the chief constable. The chief constable, with sagacity, noted there was evidently 'a little ill-feeling between the 2 men' and in the event the constable apologised to both him and his sergeant.

Another man was so lacking in vigilance he failed to see his sergeant pass him about 8 yards away, nor notice when he overtook him moments later to tell him he needed to 'keep his eyes open'.

'Am I to turn round every minute to hunt for you?' the constable asked insolently. 'What is it you are talking about, have I missed something?'[6]

Charged with using insubordinate language, he later apologised to his sergeant.

Some men never learned obedience and discipline. PC Fred Jesson of Bradford, who had previously been brought before the watch committee several times for neglecting his duty but merely cautioned, took matters too far. On 26 November 1893, at 1.45am, he was challenged as to his whereabouts for the past hour. He answered with his fists, striking the sergeant in the mouth and on the head and hurling abuse. And so ended his brief police career.

Misdemeanours were recorded in constables' disciplinary records books, and it is evident some constables found being constantly reprimanded by their superiors too much to bear.

One such example was William Beckett Scott, who was reported three times within a fortnight, twice for neglect of duty and once for being fifteen minutes late coming off duty, by sub-inspector Seth Barraclough. Constable Scott lost his temper when, once again, the sub-inspector challenged him, accusing him of not knowing what he was doing and marching him off to the main police station. Halfway there, the constable rounded on the sub-inspector, grabbed his coat sleeve, called him a 'bloody sod' and threatened to 'knock his bloody head off', before resigning and returning to his former occupation as a joiner.

Another constable who resigned in a fit of pique after being moments late at his allotted point was John Holmes. When his sergeant threatened to report him for this misdemeanour, he shouted 'You can report me and damn and bugger the bloody job', before storming off.[7]

New recruits whose previous lifestyle had included overindulging in drink found their habits difficult to break. Within a short time they found themselves dismissed for their intemperance. Some supernumeraries were struck off the list before ever becoming constables.

One was probationer constable Thomas Walton, found vomiting in the street at 1.20am. His sub-inspector enquired as to what was the matter. Thomas declared: 'I have had too much [to drink] tonight to tell you the truth and I don't care about the job so I may as well give it up.'[8] Although instructed to speak to the chief constable in the morning, he was never seen again.

Men who joined the police force as a stop-gap, perhaps in times of economic recession, and those who found the restrictions on social life and the lack of time off intolerable, left as soon as the first favourable opportunity came along.

Even then there might be consequences. Thomas Banks, eager to throw off the shackles of the police force and pursue his new career as a beerhouse keeper, was fined 22 shillings (£122.10) and ordered to pay 18 shillings costs (£100) when he started his new role before his resignation period had expired.

Others who imagined they might do better elsewhere after consideration decided to stay, no matter how irritating they found the rules.

When sub-inspector William Ackroyd found Constable Joseph Thorns under the influence of alcohol at midnight on 1 April 1888, he cautioned him not to drink any more, as he had had plenty. It being after closing hours the constable walked off, grumbling 'You know I can't get any more'. An hour-and-a-half later they met again, and Thorns, who had been evidently mulling matters over in his mind, launched a verbal attack on Ackroyd, snarling: 'You said I was drunk, well if I am then take me down. You've had your knife into me for a long time and the sooner you take it out the better. If this had been any other job than policing you'd have had to fight before now. I have 8 bloody fingers and 2 thumbs and can work for any living.'[9]

The startled sub-inspector threatened to report this outburst to the chief constable, but the tired and emotional Thorns didn't care. 'Well if you don't get me removed I'll remove myself. I'll not take your humbug; I'm a better man than you. You want a case because you haven't had one lately and you've spotted me.'[10]

Thorns was fined 5 shillings (£27.75) and suspended without pay, it not being his first offence. He returned to work, but did resign two years later in April 1890, after another fine for neglect of duty, and set himself up as a house painter.

Personnel turnover was a constant problem for all forces. Despite the objective of retaining men, the rate of resignations and dismissals was high. Lancashire Constabulary lost a quarter of its staff in the first six months of being established and even thirty years later only two-thirds of new recruits stayed longer than a year. Liverpool Borough Police had to hold interviews every Thursday in 1857 in order to keep the force's strength at required levels. The West Riding Constabulary in Yorkshire faced similar issues and was still swearing in more than ten new men each month throughout the 1880s.

As pressure increased to keep forces at full strength some men were recruited before their testimonials were fully explored. However, their unsuitability was usually uncovered within a few days, resulting in their prompt dismissal.

Certificates of character were frequently found to be forged and men who may have seemed experienced but later found to have been dismissed from other police forces (often after a very short spell), were not given a second chance. West Riding Constabulary records show one man previously in the Norfolk force had been dismissed for being 'useless', another who had worked in York was described by his sergeant as having been 'jelly'. However, Constable Richard Corcoran escaped detection and was employed for almost a month before word came that he had previously been dismissed from the Dublin police force for pawning a comrade's coat.

Some of those newly appointed were soon found to have been inveterate drunkards, or before the magistrates for assault, imprisoned for felony, or to have kept the company of notorious bad characters.

Understandably, James Devey, a tall young man from Kilkenny, Ireland, was dismissed after five days service with West Riding Constabulary when he was rumoured to be connected with the rising and troublesome Fenian movement. But it seems almost cruel to dismiss another after six days because he was found to have been considerably in debt on joining the force, or one who had been previously confined to a lunatic asylum, a consequence of a head injury sustained while on duty with the Railway Police.

Men who were found to have led dissipated lives, or were of 'very loose character', were not given the opportunity to turn their lives around in a constabulary. Others were dismissed for being a quarter-of-an-inch too short or just plainly unsuitable for the position of police constable. Standards had to be maintained.

For those who submitted to the regulations and discipline, there were opportunities for progression through the ranks.

From the outset, Bradford wanted to encourage men to strive for excellence, and vowed that men already in the force would be given preference for all future appointments of superior officers, providing they were eligible:

> *To merit promotion it is only necessary for a constable to be attentive, intelligent and sober. Diligence is always in his power, the necessary intelligence is easily acquired, and to be sober requires only a firm resolution never, while on duty, to enter a public house, or accept liquor from any person whomsoever. Nothing degrades a police officer so much as drunkenness, nothing is so soon observed by the public, and nothing exalts the character of a constable so much as a steady and uniform refusal of liquor when offered to him, even with those who, at that moment may be offended at his determination.*[11]

However, maintaining resolve and avoiding causing offence was not always straightforward, as Bradford's watch committee's minutes of 23 February 1854 highlight, when constables Huntly and Ellis were dismissed, having been off their beat and accepting drink at the house of a prominent silversmith of the town. The liquor must have flowed as both were drunk when they came off duty that morning.

The silversmith too was severely reprimanded for his behaviour. Copies of the resolution were forwarded to him, informing him of the 'committee's unanimous and entire disapprobation of his conduct in offering temptation to policemen to drink at his house'.

Surrey Constabulary was a little more prescriptive in its directions on how to obtain promotion:

Every constable must make it his study to recommend himself to notice by diligent discharge of his duties, and strict obedience to the commands of his Superiors, recollecting that he who has been accustomed to submit to discipline, will be considered best qualified to command; and as no constable can be promoted who has not a thorough knowledge of his duties and powers, and who cannot write a proper official report or letter, no matter how exemplary his conduct, he should devote every hour which he can spare from his duty to reading, writing and general improvement of his mind; he should also frequently and carefully read this Book of Instructions, in order he may clearly understand his duties, and the powers which are given to him by Law, for the efficient execution of them.[12]

Men having been supernumeraries or probationers usually entered the force as a third class constable at the lowest rate of pay, which varied according to the force. In a survey carried out in 1861 after the force had petitioned for a pay increase, Bradford's watch committee realised the constables' pay of 17 shillings (£94.35) per week (as it had been since 1848) was one of the lowest when compared with other similar-sized boroughs. After a year of service, second class constables were paid 18 shillings (£100) and first class (after a further three years' service) 19 shillings (£105.50), plus all ranks had a boot allowance of 15s 6d per year (£86).

Other ranks were similarly more poorly paid than neighbouring forces, with sergeants only receiving 2 shillings a week more than the constables they were striving to command (£11.10).

The watch committee considered the matter thoroughly and determined a course of action. The superintendents' salaries would be increased from £80 a year (£8,880) to £85 (£9,435), but only once they had held the position for three years. Inspectors would have another shilling per week and first class sergeants (in position for three years) would have an extra 2 shillings a week (£11.10). As for the constables, the watch committee considered:

> *[...] a man coming into the force raw to police duties is not worth more than 17 shillings a week for the first year's service, therefore your committee does not propose any alteration, but recommends instead of 3 classes of constable a 4ᵗʰ shall be attained by length of service and weekly wages fixed as follows:*
> *Year One 17 shillings*
> *Year Two 18 shillings*
> *Year Three 19 shillings*
> *Year Four and subsequent years 20 shillings*
> *Also a Merit Class with wages at 21 shillings, appointments to this class at the discretion of the Watch Committee for extraordinary diligence or exertion by an officer in discharge of his duties.*

This meant a constable could reach the 19-shillings class (£105.45) within two years of joining the force, rather than four, so was an incentive of sorts, although attaining the higher grade did depend on good behaviour.

When four years later they repeated the exercise, they found the police in Bradford were still paid less than men in forty-two of the fifty-seven forces surveyed. The sergeants and constables 'who did most of the work' each received a pay rise of 1 shilling per week (£5.55) – around four or five percent. Inspectors' wages were increased by 2 shillings a week (£11.10). Faring even better were the superintendents, whose £15 (£1,665) a year rise represented a whopping 17.6%.

Manchester had been far more progressive in its thinking on rewarding and retaining its workforce and established a merit class in 1845, 'with a view of increasing the efficiency of the Police Service by offering additional advantages to the well-behaved and more intelligent and efficient members of the force'.[13]

Manchester's merit class was not to be limited in numbers, but open to every constable considered deserving of the advancement. The required qualifications were that the constable had served a sufficient length of time to establish his good character, and exhibited intelligence, discretion and activity in the discharge of the duties of a police officer at all times, as well as prompt obedience to orders and a desire to promote correct discipline and to bring credit on the force. Mere length of service, even where combined with good character, was not a passport to the merit class. Nor was any single act of meritorious conduct. But once attained, the constable was entitled to wear a distinguishing badge, and presented with a small gratuity each year, providing there was no act of misconduct.

Thomas Bottomley, a well-respected and steady police constable, never disciplined before the watch committee, was not admitted to Bradford's merit class until 21 March 1872, twenty years after he had joined as a supernumerary. Perhaps an opportunity to display the required virtues or exertion never presented itself until there was a dramatic murder virtually on the doorstep of the Manningham police station on 16 February. His involvement in the discovery, in a brick-yard, of an empty purse and gloves belonging to the victim, and a tatty pair of trousers discarded by the perpetrator – who had put on the victim's new trousers – perhaps qualified as extraordinary diligence.

For some, hard-won promotion, whether to a higher class of constable, or to the next level of responsibility, was easily lost.

The West Riding Constabulary examination records detail the rise and subsequent fall of many men, which must have been somewhat demoralising.

Thomas Brannagan, who joined the force in January 1857, gained relatively quick promotion to sergeant in November 1861, and within five months was placed in the class of merit for the energy and zeal in which he discharged his duties. Evidently this was not sustained as, in December 1869, his status was reduced to first class constable. There began his rapid and continued descent until his resignation as a third class constable in July 1871.

Another constable who joined the same force in September 1858 was advanced from third to second class within eight months, but was reduced back to third class within a couple of weeks. Another year elapsed before he was once again promoted to second class, this time maintaining his grade for ten months. Over the next few years he made it as far as first class, but only for a few months at a time. Eventually he, like Thomas Brannagan, slid down the ranks, before being dismissed in November 1872.

Even exemplary constables could find themselves on a roller-coaster of promotions and demotions.

Lawrence Markey of Barnsley, previously a grinder in a foundry, was recruited as a police constable in January 1859, aged 28. Clearly a brave and hard worker, Markey was appointed to the class of merit four times for various acts of courageous conduct and was twice rewarded by the chairman of Doncaster Sessions: £2 (£222) for arresting two crooks who had stolen a gun and threatened to shoot him with it; and £5 (£555) for apprehending a soldier for felony.

The *Sheffield Independent* of 23 October 1861 reported:

On Saturday, a soldier, named Robert Cameron, pleaded guilty to several felonies, and, as reported in our columns on Monday, was sentenced to twelve months' imprisonment. The prisoner was apprehended on the 10th of August, by police constable Markey, of the West Riding constabulary. He had been absent from the Barracks on leave for several days, and had stayed longer than his pass gave him leave to do. On the night of the 9th August, he scaled the Barrack walls, and took away a variety of articles from the officers' quarters. Constable Markey found the prisoner at Beardshaw's public house [the Travellers' Inn], Ecclesfield; and the fellow, on being required to produce his pass, attacked the officer in the most furious manner with a poker, aiming several dreadful blows at him. Markey fortunately evaded the blows, and, courageously closing with his assailant, wrenched the poker from his grasp. The fellow then attacked the officer with a fender, and also with a chair; but after a desperate struggle, which lasted for upwards of half an hour, Markey succeeded in handcuffing the soldier, and lodged him in the Sheffield Town Hall. The Court, who heard the case at Doncaster, on Saturday, awarded the officer £5 for his skill and courage in apprehending the soldier, and recommended him to Colonel Cobbe for promotion. Markey was similarly rewarded for courageous conduct only twelve months ago.

Despite his seemingly good police work, within his eleven-year service, Markey was promoted and demoted more than twenty times. When he was badly assaulted in 1867, the police committee awarded him 30 shillings (£166.50), but he was made to resign on 1 November 1870.

Of course, with fewer men required in the higher ranks, senior appointments to inspector or above were more difficult to attain, especially since most superintendent positions only became vacant when the incumbent retired or died. But for the few who were promoted to senior ranks, it meant a move from the working class into the middle classes, and the financial benefits, respect and status such positions brought.

Again, Surrey Constabulary gave very clear direction for those who wished to progress into the higher ranks:

Before a constable is promoted to the rank of Inspector, he will be required to undergo an examination at the Chief Constable's office, when he must be found to possess a knowledge of such parts of the Criminal Law as refer to the duties of the police: he must also be able to write neatly and correctly from dictation, and understand the first four rules of arithmetic (simple and compound). Without the above qualifications, the Chief Constable will not promote any member of the Force, however meritorious his conduct may be in other respects. In the Police Library, (which contains upwards of 600 volumes) several educational works will be found, which will greatly assist the constable in attaining the requisite qualifications.[14]

For those constables who were capable and availed themselves of education and training, promotion to inspector in the West Riding Constabulary – a mix of rural and urban areas – typically took around twelve years, and for those who went on to be superintendents, a further six or so years.

These were ordinary men whose occupations prior to joining the force had been as labourers, farm workers, gardeners, painters and woollen industry workers. In that time their weekly wages would increase from 18s 6d (£103) to 31s 6d (£175) as a second class inspector, eventually reaching 61s 6d (£341) as a first class superintendent. Riches indeed.

Some men had a faster track to promotion, particularly if they had military experience or a better education, but life at the top may not have been all they expected.

George Sykes from Holmfirth, who had started his working life as a wool spinner before spending three years in the Grenadier Guards, joined the West Riding Constabulary aged 22, on 6 December 1856, as a third class constable. His abilities soon secured him a rapid promotion, rising to first class constable in seven weeks. By the first anniversary of his appointment he was an inspector, serving in Barnsley and Bingley for eight years, before once again earning promotion. He became superintendent of the Otley Division on 1 November 1865, later returning to Barnsley where he was warmly welcomed.

There he remained until April 1884, discharging his 'onerous, and often unpleasant, duties with great satisfaction, even to those who were most likely to have looked on him with great disfavour' (*Sheffield Independent*, 5 May 1884).

When the chief clerk at constabulary headquarters in Wakefield retired, Chief Constable Captain Russell recommended George Sykes for the role and for William Smith Gill of Sheffield to take over Sykes' superintendent's post in Barnsley.

At the end of April, George Sykes moved into the police residence at Wakefield with his wife to take up his new duties. Some had noticed, even in the weeks before his promotion, that Sykes had seemed to be in indifferent health and much depressed in spirits. He had even been off-duty for a short time, spending time in Scarborough to recuperate. Moving from Barnsley, where he was well-known and respected, seems to have had further detrimental effect on his well-being, despite the obvious pecuniary benefits of his promotion. His spirits and health deteriorated and on 4 May he arose at around 7am and went into the back garden. His invalid wife later awoke and, realising her husband had not returned to the bedroom, called for her sister, Miss Garbutt, to search for him. Entering the back yard, Miss Garbutt, to her horror, discovered a large pool of blood seeping under the outhouse door. George Sykes was found inside, having twice shot himself in the head with the six-chambered revolver he had been carrying with him for a few weeks.

That he had been a well-loved and respected police officer was evident as three different sections of the Barnsley community had already raised subscriptions towards making presentations to him and his wife as a mark of their esteem. His own officials and constables, by whom he was greatly beloved, had raised over £30 (£3,330) with which to buy him a beautiful case of cutlery and Mrs Sykes an equally suitable present. The magistrates, gentry and tradespeople had also subscribed liberally to a fund, reaching several hundred pounds. Even the innkeepers, beerhouse keepers, and the trade generally were due to present an independent testimonial to show their regard.

His widow was granted £300 (£33,500) as a gratuity and a further sum of £98 13s 4d (£11,000) was raised by the members of the force.

William Smith Gill, son of a clothier from Almondbury near Huddersfield, previously a solicitor's clerk, joined the newly established West Riding Constabulary as a constable on 12 January 1857. Another fast-tracker, within eight months he was promoted to inspector and assistant chief clerk.

In 1862, William Gill was appointed superintendent of the Keighley Division until 1875, when he transferred to take charge of the Selby district. Clearly, he too was well-respected and regarded, as he was presented 'with a gold watch and guard, magnificent sterling silver tea and coffee services, bronze clock and tazza (a shallow bowl mounted on a foot), and a purse of 100 guineas, altogether in value over £400, by the magistrates and principal inhabitants of Keighley' (*York Herald*, 21 February 1891). His wife was also presented with a silver-mounted dressing case. After three years he moved again, this time to Sheffield (and with a handsome purse of gold from the grateful Selby population), where he stayed until 1884, before transferring to Barnsley to take over the superintendent's position vacated by George Sykes. With the sad suicide of George Sykes creating a vacancy again, it was only a month before William Gill was once more promoted – to chief clerk at the Wakefield headquarters.

On 18 February 1891, still holding the chief clerk's position, William Gill was awarded the additional responsibility of deputy chief constable of the then second largest police force in the country.

On his retirement on 1 June 1907, after fifty years of service in the same force, he was granted a pension of £400 (£44,400). His retirement after such a long and distinguished career was relatively short as he died on 17 August 1909.

Chapter 4

Police terms, conditions and expectations

The instruction book issued to every constable on appointment detailed the terms and conditions of his employment and the expectations of the role.

In addition to his pay, a 'good and becoming uniform' was provided, which he was required to keep neat and clean at all times so as not to be a discredit to the force. If the uniform was damaged in the course of duty, its repair was paid for by the force, otherwise the cost of mending any tears or marks through the constable's carelessness was to come out of his own pocket.

The uniform, costing around £5 (£555) per man, consisted of an outer great coat, a cape, another coat, two pairs of trousers, a hat, belt and armlet (to be worn when on duty). Men were either provided with boots or paid an allowance to purchase their own. The latter was preferable as the boots supplied were often ill-fitting, causing blisters and discomfort as men covered the miles patrolling their beats. To guard against the risk of being garrotted – a widespread crime of the time – the police were issued with a stock, often made of leather, to be worn around the neck. It probably served to give them a rather aloof posture.

To maintain a smart appearance, certain parts of the uniform were replaced annually.

It is evident, from an article in the *Leeds Times* in July 1877, that from time to time there was dissatisfaction with the comfort and durability of the issued uniforms. The report related to Bradford's watch committee's idea to change the system from a boot allowance to the provision of regulation boots:

> *Our readers may recollect that some time ago, when the Watch Committee thought of taking away the "Bobby's" boot money supplying them with boots instead, Policeman XYZ, a steady officer who minds his business and works his beat to perfection, took your representative into a passage one wet night, and, taking off his cape and leggings asked the "chiel (child) who tak's notes" to feel. He felt and to his surprise, found both cape and leggings were wet inside as out; they were – like many men and things – a sham, a delusion, and a snare. A sham, because they professed to be what they were not; a delusion, because they took the fellow in who trusted to them; and a snare, because they might have been invented for the propagation of rheumatism. And so thought Policeman XYZ, who said he had some awful twinges in his shoulders and his extremities. Well I do recollect the honest fellow's visage as he said "Suppose the boots should turn out like the capes and leggings?" The other night I met him again. It was one of those steady downpours that the watery saint has sent us. Looking cautiously round, though the hour was late, he said "I want to show you something sir. My sergeant will not be here just yet. If you come into this passage I will slip off one of my boots, and you can see what they are like for yourself."*
>
> *Suiting the action to the word he clanked up the passage, the plates on his boot-heels being loose, and with something that was certainly not prayer, he pulled off one of the boots, banged the sole against the wall, and casting the light from the bulls-eye of his lantern on the spot, said "Look, and you will see how beautifully the leather takes in the water and how it flies about when the boot is struck against the wall. My stockings are sopping wet and I*

sometimes fancy, when I apply my thumb to the sole of my boot, that I could send it through. Some of our fellows say these boots are grand for fine weather; one of them has kept his boots to look at, fearing to trust them on a wet night; another has had a good leather sole put on the stuff they call leather, so as to keep his feet dry; and another says he has spent 16 shillings on a new pair of boots, and does not intend to wear the regulation boots! But I cannot do that. My family takes all my brass and what am I to do, with wet feet, wet legs, and wet shoulders. God help me. Our Watch Committee must be trying to kill us before our time. I wish they would make members of the Watch Committee wear boots like these in wet weather with the men who made them walking ahead, each with a pair on his feet, then we would be satisfied that we should get boots that would, at least, keep out water."

It was true enough; as the fellow said the inside of the boots were also wet, and as he pulled the boot on and clanked down the passage we couldn't help thinking of the warning that was given when it was known these boots were to be adopted. The committee have, however, had their whim, and perhaps the regulation boots which are, no doubt, good enough for the price paid for them, have had their day. The "Bobbies" generally, and especially policeman XYZ would like to revert to the old order of things, have the boot money and shoe themselves; for what can be worse than fine weather boots for wet nights?

Failure to wear the correct uniform could mean a reprimand from the chief constable. Outer garments such as the greatcoats and capes were expected to last, but when two constables took the initiative to replace their worn-out capes with something more suitable to protect them from the persistent rain one June night in 1885, they were reported by their sergeant.

Besides keeping smart and tidy, good timekeeping was another virtue. The best proof a constable could give that his duties were not irksome to him was always to attend his relief punctually.

Even though duties may not have been irksome, they may have been wearisome and men regularly turned up late for parade through oversleeping. Without alarm clocks, ordinary people relied on a knocker-up to rouse them from their slumbers so they might hasten to their workplace. But when the knocker-up was ill and didn't turn up, a man might not wake in time to be on parade. In the case of PC John Wilson, this excuse was offered when his oversleeping meant he was more than an hour late for work.

Sometimes confusion could cause a policeman to be late for his appointed duty. Applying the strictest of timekeeping rules, Inspector Ackroyd reported constables George Fuller and Marshall Gibson for being three minutes late in delivering ballot boxes to a polling station at a school in Thornton Lane, Bradford. An over-anxious presiding officer, Mrs Hutchinson, had speedily dispatched a telegram to the town hall, before the (presumably) exasperated men turned up, having been to the wrong school.

Too much drink was a frequent cause of lateness, but rather than turn up late or unfit for night duty, Constable Summers decided not to go to work at all after a summer afternoon outing with friends. Having had too much to drink, the constable wisely stayed at home, thus avoiding dismissal, getting away with a relatively small fine of 1 shilling (£5.55).

Recognising that being insulted and encountering provocation were part of a policeman's lot, constables were explicitly urged not to act as they might as individuals, but to think of their public office.

Displays of anger, resentment and bad temper would only expose them to more insults and deprive them of the presence of mind essential for their own protection and reputation of the service. Coolness and forbearance were the watch-words if they were to gain the approval and elicit the help of the law-abiding public.

A report from the *Manchester Courier and Lancashire General Advertiser* of 13 November 1886 tells of a huge disturbance at the closing of the Liverpool Shipperies Exhibition, where several constables, having earlier been under extreme provocation, did not regain their composure and were alleged to have 'without a word being said, commenced to attack women, men, and children, indiscriminately'.

The International Exhibition of Navigation, Commerce and Industry had been opened by Queen Victoria on 11 May 1886, amid drenching rain and boisterous winds. A grand affair, it had cost £148,000 (£16,428,000) to stage and had included among its exhibits Grace Darling's rowing boat and a life-size replica of the 170-feet-tall Eddystone lighthouse. Visitors could take camel or elephant rides or watch a cigar-shaped 'captive balloon' travel vertically 250 feet every hour.

The problem started when around 50–60,000 people thronged to the event on its last day. A mixed class of folk attended, from leading Liverpool families to local and country artisans. Although the exhibition was packed, all went well until the early evening, when gangs of well-dressed drunken young men started to push and jostle their way round the gardens before entering Mr Wood's refreshment rooms. As the event came to a close and the band played the National Anthem, the inebriated crowd took up the refrain, whooping and shrieking. The employees of Mr Wood's establishment tried to close the place but those inside resisted ejection. One of the policemen inside the premises was rolled in the sawdust and doused with liquor from the glasses of the young 'swells'. A *mêlée* ensued but somehow the staff managed to pitch everyone out of the building, slamming the doors closed.

Once outside, the mob became even more excited and others joined the multitude, launching an attack on the refreshment room doors and smashing them in. The crowd was met by a line of policeman who, in response to the heavy sticks possessed by a mob of youths, drew their truncheons and inflicted heavy blows on many of the young men. The fighting was hand-to-hand and the wholesale smashing of glasses and bottles added to the confusion and hostilities.

Gentlemen rushed their screaming wives and children away to a place of safety. Emerging from the gates and into Liverpool's Edge Lane, those who had escaped the turbulence allegedly found themselves under attack by half-a-dozen or so over-excited constables. Several people were injured. One woman was struck on the head and her husband, coming to her defence, was knocked insensible.

Two of the constables were summonsed to appear before the magistrates, but the complainants could not identify their assailants. Defending the police, their barrister stated he did not doubt that on the night in question the complainants had been dealt blows by someone, but the rest of the case was a: 'trumped-up, miserable attempt to make out a case against two decent men, who happened to be policemen. There had been a rush and crush on the last day of the exhibition, and had the police not exercised their functions with a great deal of consideration, there would have been complaints long before.' (*Manchester Courier* and *Lancashire General Advertiser*, 25 November 1886.)

He claimed the policemen had performed their duties wisely and well. After a long day of arguments and counter-arguments, the magistrates judged in favour of the police and dismissed the summonses.

Since the security of life and property depended on their efficient discharge, a constable's duties were of great public importance. These duties were described as being straightforward and simple, with the law giving him large powers and ample protection in which to fulfil them – and the instruction book explicitly spelling out what those duties entailed.

It is evident by the ratio of night police to day police, and the need for night watchmen prior to professional policing, that most trouble occurred under cover of darkness.

A constable arriving on his beat for night duty was to visit every part of it immediately, and to keep going round until his duty finished in the morning. He was required to be at certain points at specified times and his sergeant would expect to meet him at that appointed time and place.

He was expected to walk his beat to a regular routine, so he might easily be found. One lack of communication and understanding led to a sergeant reporting a constable in his division, after he had 'cause to spend an hour searching for him in the darkest hours of night'. It transpired, having misunderstood his sergeant's instructions, the constable had been merely working his beat the wrong way round.

By also walking his beat during the daytime, a night constable could get to know it well, acquainting himself with the different yards and alleys where criminals could lurk, and becoming familiar with the residents and business owners so he might call on them in the event of their premises being unlocked, robbed or on fire.

Above all he was to notice all disorderly characters and disorderly houses 'in order to prevent crime by impressing bad characters with a conviction that they are known and watched by him'. As the bad habits of these characters would point them out sufficiently, there was no need to get into conversation with them, or to chat idly to any of the inhabitants.

His first task of the evening was to ensure everywhere was safe and tranquil and places closed for the night were locked. Owners of unlocked premises were to be alerted, and where buildings were already securely fastened the constable was to leave himself a sign – perhaps placing something in the keyhole – so when he made his later and frequent inspections he would notice if there had been an attempt to unlock the door.

Failure to carry out this important task could result in being brought before the watch committee for neglect of duty. Even using a bit of initiative did not suffice. One constable, having checked every interior door in a warehouse was locked, sought not to wake the owner when he found the outer door open – instead securing it with a prop – but found himself cautioned by the chief constable for his apparent carelessness.

Business premises were not the only buildings to be checked. Private homes, schools, churches and chapels too. Constable Dews was reported for failing to try the doors of the Baptist school in Bradford's Caledonia Street when, at 4.25am on 7 January 1889, his sergeant found the doors unlocked. When the caretaker was called, he admitted he had forgotten to fasten them at 10pm the previous night, but it was the policeman who paid a fine.

Forgetfulness was the order of the day it seemed, and it continued to be so.

In 1844, the chief constable in Manchester reported that during the previous year 2,798 premises had been found by the police to be open and insecure, more than seven every night. Over half of these were warehouses and shops containing property where nobody was resident, leaving them vulnerable to burglars.

Either the inhabitants of Liverpool were better at locking doors than their neighbours in Manchester, or had become better trained since the police had instilled in them the importance of security over a period of time. In 1856, there were a mere 1,465 found open, just over half the number of those in Manchester.

However, the chief constable of the Huddersfield borough police force mentioned in his annual report of 1879 that police on night duty had reported 473 instances of premises found insecurely fastened, an increase on the previous year of 165. He appealed to occupiers of premises to take care to fasten them securely, to negate the need for constables to be detained for a considerable time, either making the premises safe or finding the occupiers – the time so engaged meaning the whole of the other property on their beats be neglected. His plea must have fallen on deaf ears as the following year he reported 878 unlocked doors and, in 1881, 922. As the number of buildings grew, so did the number of premises left unlocked.

Clearly it represented quite a chore for the constables to have to check every door, and it is little wonder that some elected not to do so. Statistics from Birkenhead's annual report on its strength of force show the borough had 95 miles of streets in 1887. During the day shifts, this meant each man had around 5 miles of streets to patrol as he pounded his beat. The night shift, with thirty-five constables, had a shorter patrol of just under 3 miles each, but had to try the door of each of the 15,300 houses after lights were out – an astonishing 437 houses each on average – plus all business premises.

Some police forces introduced a key-keeping service for which they charged an annual fee, the money earned being added to a superannuation fund. Warehouse and factory owners could deposit a key at the police station after they had locked up for the night, collecting it again in the morning. That way, not only was there certainty the building was locked, but it also meant the police could have speedy access if necessary, without first having to seek out and wake the owner.

A lazy policeman could, of course, still decide to just prop a warehouse door closed, rather than return to the police station to obtain the deposited keys, thereby contravening his chief constable's orders.

Ensuring all doors were locked was not always a failsafe against burglaries. Ladders left against walls were an invitation to the felons of the towns. The police were instructed to warn people to remove them and, if they did not, to seize the ladders and place them in the pinfold. Other items left in the street and causing obstruction or nuisance could also be taken to the pinfold, and this included horses, cows, pigs, sheep and other animals wandering through the street without their owners or drivers.

Having checked properties were locked, no ladders were lying around and the streets were free from wandering livestock and stray dogs, the constables' attentions could, at last, turn to keeping order in the streets.

Chapter 5

Seeing and being seen

One of the key elements of reducing crime and instilling more orderly behaviour in the Victorian streets was the visibility of the professional police force, the aspiration being that people might conduct their lives in a more appropriate manner if they could see they were being observed.

The idea of being watched was heavily criticised. An article in the *Warder and Dublin Weekly Mail* on 24 August 1839 alluded to the new police bill getting a second reading for the new borough of Bolton in Lancashire, and seems to sum up the general feeling of many of the population:

> *Peace be with the good old days of Watch, Watch; when there was nobody to watch you – and you were permitted to go about your business of a morning without having spies upon you at every turn. In those days you did not take everybody you met for rogue, a Chartist, or a Precursor, and you had no occasion to pay a parcel of walking gentlemen to defend you from injuries which you had no cause to apprehend. But those days are gone – the watch-boxes are broken up, and the Charlies, poor fellows, all, or nearly all, gathered to their fathers! How changed are the times! We now wake and find ourselves in Whig world – when the name indeed of liberty is much in people's mouths, and we may walk abroad and suppose ourselves free – but when, at the same time, we must remark on every preparation made.*

Bolton had been recently troubled by Chartist riots and it seems the mayor, being a Chartist sympathiser, had done little to quell the rallies. It was believed had he taken proper control, the ineffectual police force might have not been shown to be quite so useless and in need of replacement by a proper force:

> *My lords, we must put an end to this system of employing men as magistrates for the maintenance of the peace who have been concerned in its violation. When we shall have taken this necessary step, we may then trust to the old constituted forms which exist in this country, and call on the people themselves to preserve the public peace, without having policemen under our noses to whatever quarter we turn.*

It was asserted that the situation should not be taken advantage of:

> *[...] to introduce a dreadful system of centralised police, which would destroy one of the best and most invaluable characteristics of English liberty, by depriving those localities of the power of managing their own police and establishing a species of domination quite as odious and mischievous as the central system in France.*

Whether the antagonists were against a completely centralised national police force, or against forces that were still locally controlled but at an increased cost to ratepayers, it is clear the police were believed to be an unnecessary evil in many quarters. It was vital, therefore, that officers conducted themselves in a way that was beyond reproach if they were to gain the respect of those over whom they watched.

Whether policing in urban or rural areas, politeness and respect for all was the maxim. Keeping in mind the public good, a constable had to treat those who asked questions of him with civility and attention and be willing to give all information in his power without delay, although he was not to enter into idle conversation with anyone on matters regarding the police service. When walking along the streets of a town he was not to shoulder anyone, but to give way in a respectful manner, keeping to the outside of the pavement during the day and next to the houses at night. Insolence and incivility would not be overlooked, nor would improper language.

On 4 November 1871, 'A Young Lady' was so displeased by the conduct of some police constables she wrote to the editor of the *Manchester Guardian*:

> *Sir, A few evenings ago myself and sister were returning home from Oxford Road by one of the carriage company's omnibuses and coming down Market Street a policeman jumped onto the step and seeing another policeman he called out to him and this was repeated until 5 of them were on the 'bus.*
>
> *The conversation was disgusting, and on my asking to get out, very rude remarks were made. We generally suppose policemen to be the guardians of decency but our experience tends rather to the contrary. The insertion of this letter in your valuable columns will exceeding oblige.*

A reply to the letter was made by Henry Robinson and Thomas McKay from Albert Street station on behalf of Manchester Police and published on 15 November 1871:

> *Sir, In your impression of Saturday 4th there appeared a letter from a young lady complaining of improper conduct on the part of some police constables when riding in an omnibus in Market Street.*
>
> *On the letter being observed by the police of the A division, a meeting was at once held and the undersigned were deputed by the meeting to investigate the case with a view of discovering the constable or constables whose imputed misconduct was felt to be a reflection upon the whole force.*

It is gratifying to us to say, and we hope it will be to the young lady to learn, that our investigation has proved successful and the offending constable has this day received well-merited punishment from Captain Palin and is now no longer a member of this force. In making this announcement we beg to assure the young lady we feel acutely the unmanly conduct she has been exposed to by one of our number disgracing his office and trust.

In future if your valuable paper is made the medium of complaints against the police they will esteem it a favour if the parties so complaining will consider it their duty, when called upon, to come forward and substantiate the charges made.

By giving the insertion to the above you will oblige those who feel it a hardship to have to bear public odium for the misconduct of others.

When Robert Peel established the Metropolitan Police Force, he stated his basic mission for the police's existence was the prevention of crime and disorder, as an alternative to repressing crime and disorder by military force and severity of legal punishment. As the public feared the deployment of the military in what were usually domestic matters, it was hoped the public would now approve of and respect the police and allow them to carry out their duties – the power of the police stemming from the consent of the public. To clearly distinguish the police as a civilian and not a military force, the uniforms were carefully designed in a neutral blue colour rather than red, the military colour of the time.

However, the police still needed to be seen as a smart and disciplined unit, and to this end maintained the practice of the constables marching behind their sergeant in single file to their respective beats before and after every period of duty.

When Captain Willis, chief constable of Manchester, visited the two London and the Dublin police forces in 1846 he reported on the general appearance of the constables of the three forces, and on their efficiency in drill. The Dublin force, he noted, was 'certainly superior either to the London Metropolitan or the City of London Forces; they are also exceedingly well-drilled'.[15]

Not only were the Dublin men well-drilled, but they were also taller, averaging 5 feet 11 inches in height. Their larger physical size and strength gave them the advantage over the men they were arresting who, realising resistance was futile, gave themselves up quietly.

In contrast to Dublin's force, 'the London Metropolitan Police Force appears to the chief constable rather to have fallen off in the smartness of appearance which they formerly possessed, or if not fallen off, they have not certainly progressed.'[16]

Willis believed this lack of general smartness was possibly attributable to the fact that the men were never obliged to practise marching once they had been appointed as constables, although this argument was countered by him noting the City of London police were even less smart in their appearance, despite having drill imposed on them for any neglect of duty. He concluded, therefore, that drill as a punishment to constables otherwise burdened with heavy duties was unlikely to increase their smartness.

The chief constable was also gratified to report the general appearance of the Manchester Police was creditable in every respect and the constables efficiently drilled, for which he claimed the credit. He did remark that the inspectors and sergeants of the Dublin force were better trained in instructing their men how to march than their Manchester peers and indicated any deficiency in that respect was to be remedied before long.

The West Riding Constabulary, also aiming to improve the smartness of the men, appointed former Sergeant Major William Robinson as an acting inspector on 28 July 1875, the day after he retired from the 2nd Battalion of the Scots Fusiliers. William had been in the army for twenty-one years and ninety-nine days, and seen action in the Crimean campaign as a 17-year-old. His military experience made him ideal for the specific role of drill instructor to which he was assigned. He was still the drill inspector for the force when he died suddenly on the streets of Wakefield on his way to work in January 1895.

As well as being visible, smart, civil and attentive, if the police wanted the co-operation of the public in their fight against crime and disorder, they also needed to be accessible and approachable, to both the public and to their superiors.

Shortly after the establishment of the borough force in Bradford in 1848, the chief constable decided that as well as the main police station in the town centre, there should be a resident day and night constable in each of the townships of Bowling and Manningham and the hamlets of Great and Little Horton. Each constable would affix a board, painted with his name and the words 'Police Constable', over the door of his house. This would be provided by the chief constable. It meant the public knew where to find a policeman whenever they needed one. Each of these districts eventually had its own police station, but not for a further ten years.

Other constables in the borough could choose where to live, but understandably this was never to be in a beerhouse or public house. A constable was to notify the police station of any change of address immediately the change had taken place. As all constables were required to be available to be called upon for duty at short notice, knowing where they lived was imperative.

Manchester had a problem since many of its constables were lodged in a straggling way across the borough. Although not a fan of the barracks system of housing police adopted by the Metropolitan Police, the chief constable did approve of the London arrangement of renting houses to be sub-let to constables. Proposing Manchester do something similar, he suggested that houses near to police stations be let to married constables, who could take in single constables as lodgers. That way the men would be brought within immediate call of the stations. Not only did it mean they could be quickly assembled in case of sudden disturbances, but also they would be easy to check up on and attend to if they called in sick. Living close to the workplace also reduced the likelihood of them being late for duty. Although this may have been perceived as an imposition by the constables, there was a security of tenure for them as the watch committee would be responsible for paying the rents – monies being recoverable from the employees' wages. All they needed to do was submit to a weekly house inspection to see they were keeping things in a clean and healthy state.

Numbers of constables on the beat and the size of the beats were also a factor in police accessibility. In some districts the beats were so large the constable might be away from portions of it for lengthy periods as he patrolled. This may have not been as much of an issue in the less populous rural areas, but in busy boroughs it might create problems.

This was highlighted once again by Manchester's Captain Willis in his comparisons of the London, Dublin and Manchester forces. The number of police in the eighteen divisions within the Metropolitan Police totalled 4,749 for a population estimated to be 2,068,100, averaging one constable for every 435 inhabitants. The much smaller City of London force with 543 men had one constable for every 230 inhabitants and Dublin had one per 357. In contrast, the four divisions within the Manchester force had only one constable for every 701 inhabitants. This 'paucity of men', as Willis described it, meant the beat sizes were too large.

The beats in populous parts of London and Dublin took between ten and twenty minutes to complete, and those in the surrounding country areas less than forty-five minutes, whereas in Manchester only eight percent of the 224 night beats took under twenty minutes to patrol and almost half were over forty-five minutes – some even longer than two-and-a-half hours. It meant that, unlike London and Dublin, where it seemed impossible any occurrence of importance could take place without the almost immediate presence of a constable, day, evening and night beats in Manchester were seldom if ever completed, especially where the numerous calls took men away to attend offences, nuisances and frequently occurring 'other special duties'.

One successful initiative was the visibility of the seven constables who patrolled the main roads leading out of Manchester. Their presence had been found to be of great service in affording protection to females and other persons returning home at night, as assaults and attempted robberies that had previously taken place had been virtually eradicated.

Of course, experienced felons intent on committing crimes could easily watch a uniformed constable on his beat and gauge whether he would be away long enough from a particular area for them to complete their nefarious deeds undetected. They were also watchful after the event, knowing they might be under suspicion or investigation. In such situations, being in uniform was perhaps a disadvantage.

For this reason some police forces had designated detectives from day one, solely for detecting and solving crimes that had been committed. Bradford appointed two detective officers at 25 shillings (£139) each per week (8 shillings more than the constables, but they had to provide their own plain clothes) whose duties were:

> *So various and of such a nature it is almost impossible to define them. In consequence of their being necessarily brought so immediately into contact with crime, in order to detect it in its multiple developments, they must be men of great experience in police matters, men of fidelity, of untiring diligence and activity, and in conduct doubly circumspect. Their principle business will be to detect crime in all its varieties; and as their duties are performed in plain clothes, they possess a great advantage over their brother officers in uniform, in watching the pursuits and haunts of all suspected persons, and all the information of this kind they obtain they must immediately give to their chief officers. They must make themselves well acquainted with the walks and beats of the police in order that assistance may be procured whenever they require it.*[17]

Clearly Bradford's chief constable, when setting up his detective team during the force's establishment in 1847, had heeded the mistakes made by earlier men.

Manchester introduced a completely separate detective division in about 1842, the same time as the Metropolitan Police established its separate detective force. In Captain Willis's first-hand investigation into the running of London and Dublin's police forces, he found the Metropolitan Police Force had had to make changes to the way its detective force worked, since it had been realised that having a totally separate detective division called on after the crime had taken place was not the best way to solve cases, nor was it good for overall morale. Constables on the beat, far better acquainted with the thieves and bad characters in their areas than the detectives, were somewhat reluctant to pass on all they knew when they perceived a detective would reap the merit and financial advantage attached to solving the crime. This delay meant parties escaped who might otherwise easily have been arrested.

The Met's new system saw six officers or constables appointed each night to do duty in plain clothes in districts where notice had been received that a robbery or other crime was contemplated, or suspicious characters had been seen about the area. The felonious parties watching the constable in uniform and waiting for him to go to another part of his beat before continuing their activities would be unaware they were being watched by the men in plain clothes – who, of course, would be on the ground, ready to make a swift arrest.

Manchester had already partially adopted a similar plan and found it beneficial both in preventing crime and apprehending offenders, as well as creating a high degree of interest in the service from the constables, who saw an opportunity to progress.

As an inducement to all constables to take an interest in the service, Manchester police later established a rule that in any case where a constable (even a perfect novice) obtained information on particular matters connected with police business, by reporting the matter to his superintendent would receive every assistance to bring the case to perfection, 'either by having an old and intelligent officer appointed to instruct him how to act, or by the personal advice and aid of the superintendents, but he will never be supplanted in the case, or have the matter placed in another's hands.'[18]

Having detectives in civilian clothes in the force created the unforeseen issue of parties unconnected with the police assuming the authority of plain-clothed constables. Manchester's watch committee soon resolved the problem by issuing warrant cards to all constables, to be carried and exhibited whenever their authority might be called into question.

So there could be no doubt in the minds of the public, the committee agreed to insert an advertisement in all Manchester newspapers:

> *The Watch Committee of the Council hereby give notice that in consequence of certain parties not belonging to the Police Force having assumed the authority of Police Constables, each member of the Force is now supplied with a Warrant Card containing his name number and the date of his appointment under the signature of the Chief Constable, and countersigned by the Superintendent of the Division of the Force he is attached. Every Officer when on duty and not wearing uniform is instructed to exhibit his Warrant Card whenever his authority to act as a Constable for the Borough is called into question. EDWARD WILLIS, Chief Constable*[19]

Chapter 6

Keeping order in the streets

Much of the disorder in the streets was the result of excessive alcohol consumption – a situation that continued to worsen.

As early as 1848, Bradford's watch committee expressed its alarm at the great increase in prostitution within the borough, believing the increase of this evil and other crimes could be traced to the high number and improper management of the beerhouses. It considered there needed to be an immediate and entire change in the laws affecting licensing and management of such houses, limiting numbers and placing them under the immediate control of the local magistracy.

The Licensing Act 1872, which expanded and amended the Wine and Beerhouse Act of 1869, sought to give more powers to the police and magistrates to prosecute those who committed alcohol-related public order offences. Its penalties were severe.

A person found drunk in the highway, public place or on licensed premises could be fined up to 10 shillings (£55.50) for a first offence. This was a high proportion of a week's wage. A second offence within twelve months could cost the inebriate 20 shillings (£111), and further offences as much as 40 shillings (£222).

Anyone being riotous or disorderly, or drunk in charge of any carriage, horse, cattle or steam engine, or in possession of loaded firearms, was liable to be arrested and fined up to 40 shillings (£222) or sent to prison for up to a month – with or without hard labour.

High penalties were introduced to discourage keepers of licensed premises from selling too much drink. A licensee permitting drunkenness or quarrelsome, violent or riotous behaviour on his premises could be fined £10 (£1,110) for the first and £20 (£2,220) for subsequent offences, and the convictions recorded on his licence. Similar penalties were imposed for licensees who served alcohol to someone already drunk.

Nor could a licensee allow his public house to be the habitual resort or meeting place of prostitutes, even if their reason for being there was not prostitution. He could allow them to stay briefly to partake of refreshment, but no longer than necessary. If he permitted the premises to be a brothel he could be fined up to £20 (£2,220) and be permanently disqualified from holding a licence to sell intoxicating liquors.

This legislation gave the licensee authority to refuse admittance to, or forcibly expel drunks and quarrelsome folk from his premises. Those refusing to go were liable for a £5 fine (£555) or imprisonment with hard labour.

However, the legislation appears to have had little effect on levels of drunkenness.

In a report in the *Observer* in February 1877, after a select committee had been appointed to look at the problems of intemperance, it was stated that publicans were 'as extreme haters of drunkenness as teetotallers themselves'. This was 'not to be doubted as the drunkard was hardly the licensed victualler's friend, being the enemy of all he came into contact with'.

The journalist mused that the select committee was unlikely to 'discover the philosopher's stone, by which a drunken can be at once changed to a sober nation', but observed the enquiry would bring valuable experiences and opinions into focus. The Bill to be introduced was to seek the transfer of licensing powers from the magistrates to the local authorities, but it was not expected to get much support. This was unsurprising when many of the justices held licences for public houses themselves. The chief magistrate of Liverpool alone owned forty-three public houses, and another seventy-two prosperous inhabitants owned more than 700 pubs and beerhouses between them.

Still, the fact that the question of the nation's drinking habits was being raised in Parliament once again was welcomed, as it proved the burning and pressing matter of the 'evil of intemperance'.

During the investigation, chaired by the Duke of Westminster, Sir John Iies Mantell, the stipendiary justice for Manchester and Salford, was questioned about the problems of drink and the number of people convicted for drunkenness. Using Salford as an example, Mantell related that between 1869 and 1876, convictions had increased from 1,189 to 3,133 with just over a quarter of them being women. Although the population had also grown, the percentage of those charged with being drunk had risen from just under one percent to almost 2.4%. There had been few new public houses opened over the period, but a thirty-seven percent increase in the number of beerhouses and off-licences.

It was conjectured that the increase in the number of places available for people to buy liquor had placed temptation in their way and led 'to temptation being fallen into'. With more off-licences, it was easy for the population to buy alcohol to consume in their own homes. Wages had been higher for a time and, therefore, 'people had been earning wages greatly beyond their proper wants, and they have had recourse to drink, and spend their money in that way.'

Despite the threat of hefty fines, there were many repeat offenders before the magistrates, one man being convicted around 170 times.

Drunkenness was also cited as the reason for an immense increase in the number of common assaults on the public, which had more than doubled.

So what was a constable to do faced with so much drunken disorderliness?

Stopping the problem at the source may have been one solution. Surrey Constabulary issued instructions that a constable must report to his superintendent 'without delay any publican or keeper of a beerhouse or refreshment house who may commit any of the offences under the Act'. The duty was taken very seriously by some. Watching for irregularities and hoping to make an arrest, shortly after the Wine and Beerhouse Act had been passed, one constable concealed himself in the branches of a tree, from where he had a bird's eye view of what was going on. Unfortunately, things did not go according to plan when he leaned over too far and 'seriously upturned himself'.

Before the Licensing Act of 1872, there were other ways of dealing with those already under the influence. Constables in Bradford were advised 'always to act with fairness but never interfere needlessly':

If a drunken person be disorderly he is to speak kindly and friendly to him and persuade him to go home. If he needs assistance he is to help him, if he requires protection he is to pass him, without murmuring, to the next constable who is to pass him in the same manner to the next and so on to convey him home, if within a convenient distance, or if otherwise to the borough police office. If however he is riotous and will not go home he is to call for sufficient assistance and to convey him with all possible care to the borough police office. He is not to be struck or ill-treated and no answer is to be made to him, however violent or abusive he may be. When he finds a person stupidly drunk he is to arouse him without any violence or uproar. If he can ascertain his residence and it be within reasonable distance he is to be conveyed home, if not he is to be taken to the police office. The same conduct is to be observed toward all, whether well or ill-dressed.[20]

This was a quiet and sensitive form of policing and one apparently adopted by PC Thomas Bottomley, a citation written when he had his portrait painted claiming he would whisper to the drunken man in the street: 'If tha' don't go home to thi wife and bairns a s'al 'av to run thee in.'

Drunken women might have presented more of a problem for PC Bottomley, though. A report in the *Leeds Times* of 25 July 1868 under the headline 'Sarah in the Net again' recounted how Mrs Sarah Harrowby stood in the dock for the seventeenth time, charged by PC Thomas Bottomley for being drunk and disorderly. Finding Sarah kicking up a disturbance outside the town's infirmary at about 7pm one Thursday evening, the constable had requested her to go away.

Refusing to move on, she had struck another girl named Sarah Northrop in the eye with her flailing arms.

In court, she cried out, 'it's a lie,':

> *[...] and it was some time before the all but perpetual motion of her tongue could be checked. The woman's clapper still went ceaselessly on, but she could not refute the officer's statement, nor when the girl Northrop appeared in the witness-box, to deny she had struck her. Amidst the noise of her tongue, she was ordered to rusticate another month in the House of Correction. Before leaving the dock, however, she wheeled round, and applied the epithet "liar" with other offensive words, to Bottomley; but was called up again, and sentenced to be imprisoned another month for her conduct in court. She then went away more quietly.*

It appears Sarah's lawlessness continued, as prison records show her committed to Wakefield Gaol for a month's imprisonment with hard labour on 28 April 1882 for vagrancy and common prostitution. She was probably instantly recognisable as the records state she had two thumbs on her left hand and a nose that had been broken. Sarah died aged 36 in 1885.

Drunken women, riotous and disorderly as they were, at least could physically be more easily overcome. However, it is little wonder that quietness and caution was advocated in the way drunken men were dealt with, as a drunk could quickly turn very nasty indeed – and his intoxicated associates could enter the affray on his behalf.

Although the evidence presented by Sir John Iies Mantell to the select committee's investigation into intemperance suggested the rough conduct given by almost every drunken person towards a policeman was not serious and determined – and therefore not classified as an assault in his figures – records from the West Riding Constabulary's examination books reveal a catalogue of sometimes appalling physical abuse sustained in the line of duty by police trying to detain drunks.

Many of the 'mere struggles with drunks' cited by Mantell were fierce, as the recorded injuries testify. Concussion or skull fractures from kicks and blows to the head, dislocated shoulders, fractured legs, kicks to 'soft tissue', kicks in the ribs and abdomen were all too frequent.

Drunks often used weapons – life preservers, knives, brickbats, bits of dross found on the ground, even the policeman's own staff – to inflict wounds, others their teeth. Records show one constable was so badly bitten his finger developed an infection and had to be amputated.

Drunken Irishmen in Batley seem to have been a regular problem, with two constables being severely assaulted by a mob of Irishmen while trying to arrest just one man for being drunk and riotous in October 1871, another two being struck on the shoulder and head and kicked in the legs by one man wielding a shovel in December 1877, and a further two being attacked by a number of them on 13 April 1878, when one constable was kicked and knocked to the floor and struck with a shovel and the other hit on the head with a poker.

Even having managed to detain a drunk and get him as far as custody, there could still be trouble. There are many examples of altercations breaking out in police stations, including that of Constable Andrew McLaren, who received a heavy blow to the head causing him to be severely concussed while trying to manhandle a drunk and disorderly James Gough into a police cell.

In contrast to the beatings they received, police were urged to take great care of prisoners once they were in custody. After a number of stupefied drunks had rolled off their wooden police cell beds and appeared in court with head wounds from hitting the hard, stone floor, the chief constable of Birkenhead requested the cells be provided with safety beds to prevent 'such circumstances in which the police might come under suspicion for using unnecessary force'.[21]

Hard, stone cell floors were also implicated in the tragic death-in-custody of Jacob Warburton, who had been so inebriated he'd had to be transported to a police lock-up in a wheelbarrow. Warburton died of inflammation of the lungs brought on by exposure to the atmosphere and through spending the night without sufficient covering on the flagged floor of the cell. The inquest stated excessive drinking of 'ardent spirits' had contributed to his demise, but was not the cause of death. The jurors recommended cells for incapables be boarded with wood, and stretchers or slings be used to transport such helpless people rather than barrows.

Riotous or disorderly behaviour was not confined to drunks. Apparently 'persons perfectly sober or not incapable of knowing what they are doing' might also behave in an unseemly way – such as 'knocking at gentleman's doors, or singing in the streets'.

A constable could politely ask them to desist, but only if their conduct was such as to give annoyance to the neighbourhood was he to call for assistance to take them to the police station. Taking people to the police office for trivial or doubtful offences was frowned upon. If the person was respectable, or his residence known, it was preferable to let him go home and await a summons to attend before the magistrates the next day. Care had to be taken that a constable could not be charged with improper interference – a witness as to his conduct was always advisable.

Aside from drunken and quarrelsome men, women of dubious repute were seemingly responsible for most other street disorders.

The constables' instruction book gave clear direction on how these women of the town were to be dealt with:

> *The constable is to hold no communication of any sort under any pretext whatsoever. He must behave towards them with a determined sternness of manner and never allow them to gather in crowds on his beat.*[22]

He was advised to keep them moving quietly along to avoid trouble and, if possible remove them from the street altogether after midnight. This would prevent much disorder and robberies:

> *They not only rob gentleman and drunken men themselves, but there is an excuse for professional thieves lurking about to plan and commit robberies.*[23]

A constable was urged to keep a constant vigilance (presumably at a distance) in order to control them, but when this failed (as it invariably did) and they behaved riotously or indecently or quarrelled amongst themselves, he could take them into custody.

Again, needless interference was frowned upon and it may be supposed that while walking their respective beats the prostitutes and constables developed a regard for each other. The prostitutes may have been rough women, but no doubt they were solicitous and enjoyed lively banter. Maintaining a sternness of manner might have proved too difficult for many police constables, as they were often fined for consorting with prostitutes or being found in a brothel. However, certain misdemeanours required a stronger course of action. One constable, with eleven years of exemplary service yet unable to resist temptation, was dismissed for having sexual intercourse with a woman in a yard at 2.45am. He was off-duty at the time.

The case of one drunken sailor who fell prey to Kate Wilson, a girl of loose character, was described in the newspapers when he reported having been robbed in Leeds. Thomas Roberts, the captain of a vessel called the *Lord Worsley*, which he plied between Louth and Leeds, arrived in town one Tuesday night in October 1870. Having left his craft in the River Aire:

> *Roberts came upon the fair "craft" in question in the delightful neighbourhood of the Calls. Kate requested him to give her a penny, and he consented to do so if she would gratify him in his immoral purpose. Roberts, who acknowledged having had three glasses of beer, followed her up a yard near the Corn Exchange.* (*Leeds Times*, 22 October 1870.)

While they were 'in company', Kate robbed him of two £5 notes and a sovereign before running away. She escaped the clutches of a passing policeman, but an alert detective, hearing a rumour, later found her in the York Tavern and she was taken into custody. She was tried at the Borough Court and it was determined she had taken the money in a fit of temptation after Roberts had made his improper overtures. She was sentenced to six months with hard labour and warned any further offences would result in penal servitude.

The activities of disorderly women were not confined to the hours of darkness, however, as this report about two serial offenders in the *Leeds Times* of April 1880 reveals:

> **Disorderly Women**. *On Tuesday, at the Borough Court, Mary Ann Mullaney, nineteen, Jackson's Alley, and Kate Conlan, thirty-three, Cropper Lane, two women who have on many occasions appeared before the magistrates, were charged with collecting a crowd, and causing a disturbance by fighting together in Westgate, Bradford on Wednesday afternoon. The charge was proved by police constable Brame, and as Mullaney had been eleven times, and Conlan twenty-four times, previously convicted, they were each committed to gaol for one month with hard labour.*

Although a constable was warned against intervention where his actions might not be welcomed, or make things worse, his job was to preserve the peace. It meant where disorderly behaviour was likely to escalate and a fight, affray or riot to ensue, it was his duty to prevent such things by timely interference. Judging the difference between 'needless' and 'timely' interference was something that came with experience. And any interference carried the risk of the constable being assaulted.

The recommended course of action in cases of fighting was to disperse the parties before angry verbal exchanges turned physical. But where a fight had already broken out the police officer had the more difficult task of breaking up the fight and sending people on their way.

Such parties found the police 'obnoxious' and the constables' instruction book urged individual constables to be cautious and to 'spring their rattles to collect assistance, then go forward resolutely and keep together until the crowd have dispersed'.[24] The thin blue line.

Anyone assaulting a police officer, or in such a homicidal passion as to threaten the life of another, or who had committed a violent assault on another, was to be arrested and charged. However, if there was no visible evidence of an assault, such as blood or wounds, and the parties known to each other, the constable was advised not to interfere.

The constable could give chase and follow the offender anywhere and into any house, breaking open the door – especially if manslaughter or murder had been committed, or there was violent affray – and act decisively and without hesitation to prevent bloodshed. Nevertheless, he had to avoid being impetuous and be convinced his actions were necessary before resorting to 'such an extremity', and in cases of 'trifling assaults' forbearance was encouraged.

One constable's interference in a fight resulted in both him and his colleague being brutally assaulted. Since the main perpetrator escaped and was never brought to justice, PC Inglis probably wished he had heeded the instruction book's advice and not interfered, as this extract from the *Leeds Times* of 15 August 1874 relates:

> ***Murderous Assault on the Police***. *On Monday, at the Borough Court, two men, named Joseph Wright, bobbin turner, and Joseph Demaine, woolsorter, were charged with having on Tuesday, the 4th instant, in White Abbey Road, Manningham, brutally assaulted PC Inglis when in the execution of his duty, and rescued a prisoner, and also with having at the same time assaulted PC Bottomley. Manningham Tide was celebrated partly on that day, and there, as usual, amusements were carried on near the Lower Globe Inn, and at no great distance from there two men were engaged in an earnest fight, one of them having even his shirt off, in the middle of a dense population, and with a crowd around them. Inglis saw this, and went towards the combatants, and in the face of the crowd, who would not, of course, lend him any assistance, succeeded in seizing the one minus the shirt, and placed the handcuffs on his wrist, holding him by the other. When near the gates*

of the works of James Wilson and Sons, the prisoner Wright came up, and rescued the prisoner from Inglis, and Bottomley at the same time was struck, and knocked down, but by whom he could not exactly say, only when he got up the prisoner Demaine threw himself before him in a fighting attitude. Wright, said Bottomley, commenced it – but for him nothing would have taken place. When cross-examined by Mr Terry, for Demaine, Bottomley said he saw the prisoner (Demaine) in the crowd taking an active part before a blow was struck, and he also saw him strike Inglis, who had to be taken home in a cab. Mr Sumner, book-keeper at Messrs. James Wilson and Sons, also said he saw the prisoners in the crowd taking part in the fight and Inglis was so badly maltreated he had to be removed. A Mrs Waugh, who spoke with high spirit, said when Inglis was taking away his prisoner Demaine came to him, and, swearing loudly, said he should not take him, and then struck the officer two or three times and knocked him down; and she also saw Inglis felled by Wright, and amidst all the shirtless prisoner was rescued and got away, carrying the handcuffs with him.

This evidence of Mrs Waugh was further corroborated by a young man whose name we could not catch, but he fully implicated both prisoners in the murderous assault; and it fully deserves the name, when Inglis was struck senseless, and had to be removed, first into a house and then home, by the battering upon him of two powerful men, simply anxious to see some more fighting. Mr Terry spoke strongly in favour of Demaine; and called a retired woolstapler and a shopkeeper to speak of his previous good character – one of them having known him for fifteen years – and to ourselves personally, even the police said he had hitherto conducted himself properly. Little, however, was said by anyone in favour of Wright, who, we understand, never misses an opportunity of abusing the

police. It was also in favour of Demaine that he gave
himself up. The sentence on each was two months to the
House Of Correction.

Who the stripped fighters were we do know not, and we
understand the prisoners were also ignorant of them; but
we have been told that the one rescued by Wright and
Demaine from Inglis found his way to Shipley, where some
blacksmith knocked the Bradford handcuffs from his wrist
and thus set him free.

Fire was another hazard the police had to regularly contend with, since responsibility for firefighting generally came under the remit of the chief constable of the police force who nominated certain sergeants and police constables to be instructed in the use of fire engines. These men were paid a bonus for attending fires, and in Bradford this was 2 shillings (£11) for the first hour, 1 shilling (£5.55) for the second hour and 6d (£2.77) for every subsequent hour, with refreshments provided by the chief constable.

Those constables trained as firemen were issued with printed instructions, and were required to repair immediately to the spot of any fire, whether on or off-duty – returning to their respective beats (or home) once the fire was extinguished. Off-duty fire constables were to let the nearest policeman know their whereabouts in case they were required.

Since the first necessity at a fire was water, the police were to acquaint themselves with the location of the water plugs or fire hydrants on their beats, to know where all tanks and pumps were kept, and to know where the water turners lived.

The horse-drawn fire engine was usually kept in a building adjacent to the police station, with two or three horses always available to pull it. In Bradford, the hose appears to have been kept separately, as a light handcart for conveying the fire hose to the engines was requested as part of the police office furniture.

The discovery of a fire always needed immediate and urgent attention. A constable was to spring his rattle and cry 'FIRE', alerting any residents if the fire was at a house. If he doubted he could put out the fire singlehandedly, the constable was to run and run, knocking on doors and telling every other constable coming to his alarm which street the fire was in and the nature of the property. He was to do this briefly and without stopping for one moment. He was not to pass the message to someone else to carry. Only if he had far to run and was tired could he forward the alarm to a fresh constable once he was halfway, and even then he was obliged to keep on his course as fast as possible in case the message should miscarry.

Once at the fire station he was to render all his assistance in getting the engine ready before hitching a ride back to the fire, showing the driver the shortest route.

The other constables now on the alert were to call up all firemen and water turners on their respective beats and run to the extremities of those beats to spring their rattles to convey the message to the next man, who in turn would do the same. This was the most effective way of ensuring every constable in a town was aware of a fire and its location within a very short space of time. Any constable neglecting this important duty was likely to be severely punished.

It was surely a relief when the installation of telegraphy equipment in 1878 meant a constable had simply to run to the nearest police station, from whence a telegram could be sent to the town hall asking for the fire brigade to attend to matters.

Of course, the shouting and rattling alerted the locals. This included the thoughtless drunks who might enter a blazing building, and thieves, who might risk carrying out little looting. And naturally a crowd of onlookers nearly always attracted pickpockets.

Fires posed a great danger to police and public, and individual constables often received a monetary rewarded from the watch committee where their diligence had prevented potential disaster.

When fire broke out at a hotel in Harrogate in March 1864, Inspector Howard, one of the first on the scene, entered the building to try and discover the fire's origin. In doing so he was overcome and fell insensible to the floor. Nothing could be seen or heard of him, so at great personal risk, PC Richard Wrathall boldly and determinedly

79

searched for the inspector, eventually dragging him out from his perilous position. For this act of gallantry, the police committee rewarded him with £2 (£222) and his chief constable promoted him to the class of merit – adding a further shilling a week to his wage.

PC Richard Burniston was in the right place at the right time when, on passing Wentworth Castle on the night of Monday 3 February 1873, he noticed a flickering light, growing in size in an upstairs room. Wentworth Castle, a palatial country house near Stainborough, Yorkshire, had been left in trust for Frederick Vernon Wentworth, a landed proprietor from Staffordshire, and he was in residence at the time.

Burniston at once rang the outside fire bell but, as it had no effect in rousing the occupants, broke down a door to gain entry to the house. Eventually he managed to wake the deeply slumbering household who, led by Frederick Wentworth, took prompt action. The house's plentiful supply of water, supplemented by two small local fire engines and the energetic endeavours of the inhabitants, prevented the fire from spreading from the storeroom where it had started. By the time the larger fire engines from Barnsley arrived, the fire was under control. Once extinguished it was discovered a beam across the chimney stack had ignited, setting fire to antique furniture above it, which in turn burnt the floor and the ceiling rafters underneath. But for Burnsiton's diligence, foresight and efforts, the mansion would probably have been destroyed and he was personally thanked by Mr Wentworth and handsomely rewarded with £50 (£5,550) – a year's wage.

Keeping order in the streets also included ensuring they were free from nuisance and hazard.

This was generally the duty of the police sergeants who were expected to report on all street nuisances, including the state of the pavements and footpaths. Unlit lamps, unswept streets and any obstructions or damages incurred were duly noted. If the sergeant spotted anything likely to inconvenience the public, or anything irregular or offensive, he was bound to report it to the first officer visiting him, so it could be attended to.

Sewers, however, were the responsibility of the constables who, in times of rain, were to make sure the sewer grates were clear, lifting the grating if a cloudburst threatened to flood the streets.

The poor state of the roads and drains caused many accidents, including one in which Mr William Ellis of Japan Street in Bradford was almost buried alive when a drain he was trying to unblock outside his home caved in. Fortunately, the neighbours were able to locate a policeman quickly and assisted PC Thomas Bottomley in successfully extricating Mr Ellis from his temporary tomb – apparently, none the worse for his involuntary interment.

The discovery of dead bodies in the streets must have been a regular occurrence since an instruction was issued by the chief constable of Bradford that in cases where persons were found 'supposed to be dead', a constable was to have the body examined by the nearest available surgeon. If the person was indeed dead (and not just dead drunk), the body was to be removed to the 'place at the Workhouse, which is provided for the purpose'. An application to extend this particular dead house was made in 1852, when it was described as being only 3½ yards square.

As well as the workhouses and asylums, many police stations also incorporated a dead house where corpses might be kept until a post-mortem could be carried out and causes of death and any criminal involvement established.

Early one Sunday morning, just as he was due to come off his night duty, PC Thomas Bottomley discovered the body of a man lying face down at the foot of a quarry in Whetley Hill, Manningham. Although quite rigid when discovered, the body still had some warmth about the chest. Who he was and how he came to be there were mysteries and he was removed to the dead house. Eventually, the man was identified as 41-year-old James Lawson, a cork-cutter who lived some distance away in Girlington. During the subsequent inquest, the coroner learned the deceased had been heard by a gentleman who resided in Salt Street at about 2am. At that time, someone was entreating him to shut up and go home, but the 'deceased seemed indisposed to listen to the advice, and took his own way alone'. Prior to this he had been seen near brick-kilns in the same neighbourhood and, informing some boys he had lost his way, had tipsily rolled on. Perhaps trying to find a shortcut home in the dark, James Lawson wandered over the many large heaps of stones around the private quarry boundary until he plummeted 32 feet, head first, to his death, leaving a widow and four children without support.

Constables working the day shifts encountered different issues to those of their night shift peers and this required an alternative approach. With the public eye on them in their instantly recognisable uniforms, politeness and civility was even more important than at night, and they were advised to be circumspect in their interaction with the populace.

Rather than constantly patrolling the whole beat, the day constable was stationed in a particular street where he might be readily found by those who wanted him.

His first task when going on duty was to check the streets where there were business premises, see that everything was in order and have a brief handover from the night duty constable. This round was to be repeated where a neighbourhood was not frequented by people at work, especially on Sundays in districts inhabited by genteel folk – since many thieves took the opportunity to commit robberies while people attended church or chapel.

Once his initial round had been accomplished, the constable was to walk up and down his street 'rather quickly'. The adjoining streets were also his responsibility, but only to be entered when called upon to do so and then 'not to remain in any of them a minute longer than absolutely necessary'.[25]

Like his night colleagues, the day constable was to consider himself responsible for keeping good order in the streets on his beat, and the Town Police Clauses Act 1847 gave him the authority to take action against a host of nuisances that were likely to prevent good order being maintained.

There were penalties in the form of fines or up to fourteen days of imprisonment for any person who, in any street, committed certain offences that caused the 'obstruction, annoyance, or danger to the residents or passengers'.

The long list of offences included:

- Allowing unmuzzled ferocious dogs to be at large or urging any dog or other animal to attack, worry or put in fear any person or animal.
- Slaughtering or dressing cattle in the street, unless the cattle had met with an accident and for reasonable cause or public safety ought to be killed on the spot.
- Not keeping carts, wagons and carriages to the left or nearside of the streets when meeting other vehicles, or obstructing the street and wilfully preventing any person or carriage from passing.
- Furious driving or riding of carriages or horses.
- Allowing a public carriage, sledge, truck or barrow, with or without horses, or any beast of burden, to stand longer than necessary for loading or unloading goods, or for taking up or setting down passengers (except hackney carriages, and horses and other beasts of draught or *burthen*, standing for hire in any place appointed for that purpose by the commissioners or other lawful authority).
- Wilful interruption or obstruction of any public crossing, footpath or public thoroughfare by means of any cart, carriage, sledge, truck or barrow, or any animal or other means.
- Riding or driving a horse or any other animal and driving any cart or carriage, sledge, truck or barrow upon any footway of any street.
- Placing or leaving any furniture, casks, tubs, baskets, pails or buckets, goods, wares or merchandise, or placing and using any stands, stools, benches, stalls or show boards on any footway.
- Allowing any blind, shade, covering, awning or other to project over or along any such footway, unless such item be 8 feet in height from the ground.
- Placing any goods, wares or merchandise so they project into or over the footway or beyond the line of any building so as to obstruct or inconvenience the passage of any pedestrian.

- Rolling or carrying any cask, tub, hoop or wheel, or any ladder, plank, pole, timber or log of wood along any footway, except for the purpose of loading or unloading any cart or carriage, or for crossing the footway.
- Placing lines, cords or poles across any street, or hanging washing thereon.
- Wilful and indecent exposure with the intent to insult females.
- Publicly offering for sale or distribution, or exhibiting to public view any profane book, paper, print, drawing, painting or representation.
- Singing of profane or obscene songs or ballads, or using profane or obscene language.
- Wanton discharge of any firearm, or throwing stones or other missiles, making bonfires and throwing and setting fire to any firework.
- Wilfully and wantonly disturbing any inhabitant, by pulling or ringing any door bell, or knocking at any door, and wilfully and unlawfully extinguishing the light of any lamp.
- Kite-flying or making slides on ice or snow.
- Beating or shaking any carpet, rug or mat (except door mats, beaten or shaken before the hour of eight in the morning).
- Fixing or placing flowerpots or boxes on upper window ledges without sufficiently guarding the same against being blown down.
- Leaving open any vault or cellar, or the entrance from any street to any cellar or room underground, without a sufficient fence or handrail.
- Leaving open areas, pits or sewers open without sufficient light after sunset to warn and prevent persons from falling there into.
- Throwing or laying any dirt, litter or ashes, or nightsoil, or any carrion, fish, offal or rubbish, on any street, or causing any offensive matter to run from any manufactory, brewery, slaughter-house, butcher's shop, or dunghill into any street – unless for treating frost to prevent accidents.

- Keeping pigsties to the front of any street if not shut out by a sufficient fence or wall, or keeping pigs in or near any street so as to be a common nuisance.

Again, unnecessary interference was advocated, with first offenders receiving a warning. Those who persisted were likely to receive a summons.

One 'Loathsome Old Brute', John Warhurst, a shoemaker from Lambert Street in Sheffield, appeared in the dock in his shirtsleeves in July 1881, charged with indecent conduct for the umpteenth time. He had been found sitting against the wall of the Queen Street schoolhouse, exposing himself to passers-by (with intent to insult ...). In court the chief constable reported the man had already served twenty-one months in total for the same sort of conduct. He told Warhurst: 'It is impossible to find words to describe the loathsomeness of your character. I suppose you are past shame. It seems it is your regular habit. You are simply a loathsome old brute, and you will be sent to prison for three months, and we are sorry that is the most we can give you.' (*Sheffield Daily Telegraph*, 9 July 1881.)

As well as a list of offences likely to be committed on a regular basis, keeping good order involved driving away any 'beggars, ballad singers, gamblers and persons selling fruit or other articles in baskets'. If they refused to move on or returned frequently, the constable was obliged to seize their property and take it to the police station. The miscreant would usually be required to attend before the magistrates the following day and could find himself taken into custody for begging, behaving indecently or obstructing the thoroughfares.

Sadly, begging was a way of life for many, and the courts had a regular stream of cases every week reported in local newspapers. The *Leeds Times* of 3 April 1880 carried an account of four men, all brought before the morning session charged with being prowling beggars.

One, a cart driver 'rejoicing in the honoured name of Lord Nelson', had been apprehended by PC Thomas Bottomley at 8.30pm on Sunday evening, when he had with him around half-a-stone of bread. The chief constable condemned the practice of men going about begging, it being especially objectionable on Sunday nights when many people were at chapel. There had also been two or three robberies at the same time, which led the mayor to observe that 'begging might be a cloak for a worse crime' – but on this occasion the prisoner was discharged.

Two other Sunday night beggars, Samuel Harding, 16, and John Illingworth, 14 (and already a tramp), were discharged with a caution, it being their first offence.

The court was less lenient in its dealing with Robert Capstick, also known as Joseph Sutcliffe. The 41-year-old labourer had thirteen previous convictions, and for his latest offence of begging at one o'clock on Saturday afternoon he was sent to gaol for a month with hard labour.

Wanderers were another issue to be dealt with. In the countryside particularly, as rootless people tramped from place to place in search of work or other means of making a living, they might be found lodging in barns or outhouses, carts or wagons or in the open air. Without visible means of subsistence and unable to give a good account of themselves they were liable to be placed under arrest without a warrant.

Samuel Wright was brought before the Bradford magistrates charged with wandering the streets at an untimely hour. The respectable, but poor, poking-mechanic, bitterly conscious of his position, wept in the dock as he related his story. Having been previously employed in Sheffield, but laid-off through a downturn in work, he had sought work in Manchester. That had been fruitless so he had travelled to Bradford. Having no friends in the town he had been advised to go to the workhouse, but was refused admission as it was too late to get in, and when he asked where he should go was told to 'go to the Devil'. The magistrates discharged him, giving the police instructions to try to put him in a way of obtaining employment.

The reluctance of the guardians of the Bradford Workhouse to admit paupers after the hours of darkness seems to have been an ongoing issue for the police. In June 1879, the watch committee held an interview with a deputation of the guardians 'in consequence of the difficulty experienced by the police in obtaining for vagrants and destitute persons admission to the workhouse after the usual hour of closing'. The meeting's purpose was to induce the guardians 'to make arrangements whereby the above difficulties might be obviated'.

After more than six months' deliberation, the watch committee received a letter from Mrs Darlington, clerk to the guardians, stating a bell had been placed at the entrance to the workhouse to allow communication with the porter after the closing of the gates, and stating arrangements had been made whereby the necessity for sending a vagrant applying for admission without a ticket away from the workhouse to obtain such ticket would be avoided in future.

Mrs Darlington was a stickler for rules. Ten years later, still in her powerful post, she complained when the police surgeon sent destitute Ellen Dooley, earlier taken into custody for drunkenness, to the workhouse. Seemingly the indignant Mrs Darlington had found Ellen was not destitute as she had £3 15s 6d in her possession (£420). The matter was deferred for further inquiry.

Crippled and maimed people who begged for alms, or those who fraudulently endeavoured to procure charitable contributions, would be removed from the streets. Fortune-tellers and anyone deemed to be a lunatic could also be apprehended in the name of keeping good order in the town.

The workhouse guardians did not approve of this either and once again Mrs Darlington complained when the police sent an alleged lunatic and a prostitute suffering from disease to the workhouse. Perhaps she would have preferred they be imprisoned rather than trouble her.

For those unfortunates who had no means of supporting themselves before they were convicted, life after serving a custodial sentence was often even tougher than before. Occasionally the magistrates would show glimpses of compassion.

Edward Connolley, 'a miserable-looking Irishman, who was ill-clad and of advanced years', had spent two months in Wakefield Gaol prior to his nine months on the road seeking work, before desperation compelled him to start knocking on doors to solicit alms. Unfortunately, one of the doors he knocked on was the home of PC Surfleet, and Connolly found himself facing a prison sentence once again. In court, he told the bench he was in very low circumstances and it was the first time he had sought help. Colonel Pollard, chief magistrate, observed that the defendant's appearance showed he was not a 'professional tramp', and trusting he would not offend again, he was discharged.

Of course, many did re-offend. In 1869, the Habitual Criminals Act was passed. It required any person convicted of a felony (but not sentenced to penal servitude) be subject to police supervision for seven years, to ensure he was making an honest living. The Prevention of Crimes Act of 1871 added to the police powers in that anyone who had been issued a ticket of leave could be brought before the magistrates and returned to prison if the police suspected bad behaviour. This was an early parole system.

A register of every person convicted of a crime in Great Britain was set-up and kept in London, housed at Scotland Yard.

With the aim of trying to rehabilitate offenders, the chief constable of the Huddersfield borough force issued this statement in his annual report of 1879:

> *In many cases when persons who have been convicted for felony are discharged from prison they are without money or any means of earning a livelihood, their character is gone, and they cannot, consequently, obtain work. Thus strong temptation is placed in their way to commit new offences in order to obtain food. With a view of lessening this evil the police use every effort to obtain suitable employment for these unfortunates, and it would materially assist them if employers of outside labour or of work people in places where there is little opportunity to steal, would, when in want of either male or female labourers, communicate with the chief constable. Such persons, when engaged at work obtained for them by the police, are carefully supervised, and, being as far as possible restrained from frequenting their former associates, prove in many cases to be honest and reliable servants. (Huddersfield Chronicle, December 1879)*

Chapter 7

Fighting crime

Keeping order and preserving peace on the streets was one matter; fighting crime and protecting property was another, requiring more zeal, courage and intelligence. Not only was a constable expected to be constantly on the move and on the alert, but also to exercise his mind in the prevention and discovery of felonies. He also put himself in great danger. A single policeman, with just a staff and a pair of handcuffs, was often no match for a crook determined to make a getaway. A policeman's lot was not a happy one.

In the days before whistles became more widely used – in Bradford this was as early as 1856 when the chief constable ordered ten dozen at 8d each (£3.70) to replace the sticks for signalling, but elsewhere this was much later – the stick, rattle and voice were the only ways in which a constable could summon help from his fellow officers.

In cases of emergency such as riots, fires, violent assaults or robberies, he was to spring his noisy rattle and hope assistance would come quickly. A more discreet way of communicating with colleagues was through the tapping of a stick on the pavement three or more times if urgent assistance was required, perhaps in the case of quietly staking out robbers before they committed their felony. On hearing three taps, a constable was to respond immediately by hurrying to the tapper in great haste.

If he heard only two taps, this was the signal he was wanted somewhere, perhaps if his sergeant was trying to locate him to ask if all was well. When only a single tap was heard he was to respond with a single tap to let the officer tapping know his location and that he was on duty. This was probably a less than effective way of communicating against the loud background hubbub of the Victorian streets, so the police must have welcomed the advent of the whistle. Unnecessary tapping was not permitted.

The crimes and offences dealt with by the police were broadly defined as either felonies or misdemeanours – terms dating back to the Middle Ages, with a constable not needing a warrant for arrest if he saw a felony being committed or suspected someone was about to commit a felony.

Felonies were serious crimes and could result in forfeit of life. The most serious felonies were, of course, murder, attempted murder or manslaughter, but felonies included rape, assaulting with intent to rob, cause grievous bodily harm or to escape detention, arson, housebreaking, theft and robbery, receiving stolen goods, and many other offences meeting these broad descriptions.

In his role as a crime prevention officer, a constable could arrest a person if he was threatening the life of another or had housebreaking implements such as crowbars, Lucifer matches, gunpowder, pick-locks or stolen keys in his possession, or was armed with 'any gun, pistol, cutlass, bludgeon or other offensive weapon'.

However, a constable was to judge a person's intent from the situation and his behaviour before charging in and making an arrest. His duty bound him to 'watch with anxiety the movements of all suspicious-looking persons who enter into or pass through his beat, and if he sees them looking about or trying doors or whistling what is called the "prig's whistle" he is to question and examine them. If it be an improper hour, or if they fail to assign a proper reason for being there, he is to arrest them'.[26]

In the cases of notorious thieves, or where the felon was seen attempting to pick pockets, no doubt would exist. But it was usually better to first watch the suspected person closely in order to discover his plot.

The constable could also apprehend anyone he found concealed apparently for dishonest purposes – in yards, in stables, in empty houses, in outbuildings or up dark alleyways.

A person could also be arrested if a third person charged a suspect

Charley Rouse, nightwatchman, with his cutlass, lantern and stick. (Courtesy of Kent Police Museum)

Slaithwaite lock-up. Paid for by subscription in 1834 but allegedly never used.

Truncheons. 1863, Manchester Borough Police, 1825 and 1815, parish constables.

Holmfirth's lock-up – Th'Owd Towser.

Frederick Goodyer, Leicester's first police inspector. (Courtesy of Hinckley Past & Present)

Captain Edward Willis, chief constable of Manchester and later Inspector of Constabulary. (Courtesy of GMP Museum)

Merit Badge, to be worn on the constable's sleeve.

Cambridge Borough Police Force, 1865. (Courtesy of Cambridgeshire Police Museum)

A superintendent making his rounds by conveyance. Many superintendents sustained injuries alighting carelessly from their vehicles.

Manchester Police 1880s.
(Courtesy of GMP Museum)

MANCHESTER

CONSTABULARY FORCE.

CONSTABLES'

GUIDE.

MANCHESTER:

H. BLACKLOCK AND CO., PRINTERS, ALBERT SQUARE.

1882.

Front page of the 1882
Manchester Constables'
Instruction Book.

MANCHESTER CONSTABULARY FORCE.

————:o:————

CONSTABLES' GUIDE.

————:o:————

You are appointed under the Municipal Act, 5th and 6th, William IV., by the Watch Committee of the City of Manchester, as a Constable for the City, and for the Counties of Lancaster and Chester.

CONDITIONS OF SERVICE.

The following are the Conditions of Service upon which men are admitted and retained as Constables in the Constabulary Force of the City of Manchester :—

1.—Each man shall deposit with the Chief Constable his testimonials of character, which shall be held at the entire disposal of the Watch Committee, and be forfeited in case of dismissal.

2.—He shall devote his whole time to the service ; shall be engaged in no other trade, occupation, or calling.

3.—He shall serve and reside wherever he is appointed.

4.—He is promptly to obey all orders which he may receive from the persons placed in authority over him.

5.—He shall not, upon any occasion, or under any pretence whatsoever, accept money, or anything in the shape of fee, present, or reward, without reporting the same for the approval of the Chief Constable.

6.—He shall at all times appear in his complete uniform, unless when leave is given him to wear plain clothes.

Bullseye lantern.

Second page of Constables' Instruction Book.

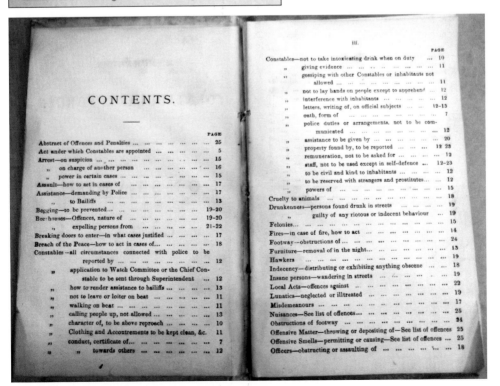

CONTENTS.

iii.

Contents of Constables' Instruction Book.

Newton Heath officers – very smart looking.

Two Cambridgeshire constables. (Courtesy of Cambridgeshire Police Museum)

Rochdale detectives. Not quite blending in to the background. (Courtesy of GMP Museum)

John Holgate, chief constable of Bolton Borough Police. (Courtesy of GMP Museum)

Police station cells, Manchester.

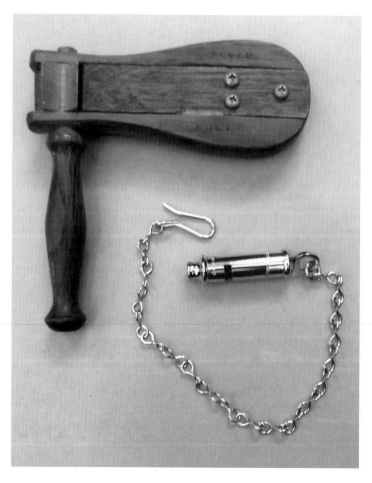

Rattle and whistle – the early means of communication. Constables had to provide their own sticks.

Dashing to a fire. (Courtesy of GMP Museum)

Handcuffs. In order to restrain a prisoner the constable had to snap the left-hand side of the cuff around the prisoner's wrist and hold on to him using the right-hand side of the device.

Cambridge officers, 1880s. (Courtesy of Cambridgeshire Police Museum)

Kent officers, 1898. (Courtesy of Kent Police Museum)

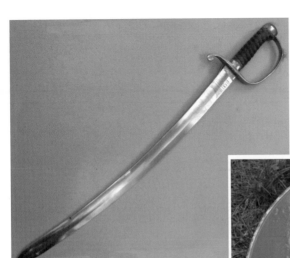

The cutlass – to be issued and used only in dire situations.

Plaque that marks the site of the 1867 Fenian ambush, Hyde Road, Manchester.

Fenian Ambush
(September 1867)
Site of the rescue of two Fenian prisoners. Following the shooting of a policeman three of the rescuers were executed at the last public hanging in the Manchester area.
(November 1867)

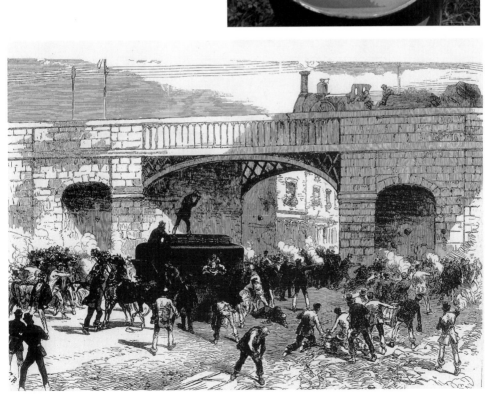

Etching of the Fenian Ambush 1867.

Tankersley police and colliery officials, 1893 Miners' Strike. (Courtesy of National Coal Mining Museum for England)

Cambridge Borough Police at Peterborough show, 1895. (Courtesy of Cambridgeshire Police Museum)

Oldham Jubilee Day, 1899. (Courtesy of GMP Museum)

Manchester Peelers. (Courtesy of GMP Museum)

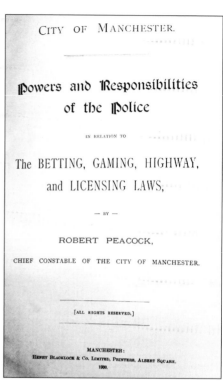

The author's great-great-grandfather, PC 50 Thomas Bottomley, 1891. (Courtesy of Bradford Police Museum)

Peacock's lectures in 1899.

Charles Malcolm Wood, chief constable, Manchester 1879-1896. (Courtesy of GMP Museum)

Robert Peacock, Manchester's longest serving chief constable. (Courtesy of GMP Museum)

Horse ambulance. (Courtesy of GMP Museum)

Swansea Police Band. (Courtesy of South Wales Police Museum)

Police Sports Day. A dash for the line. (Courtesy of GMP Museum)

Kent Police cycle section. (Courtesy of Kent Police Museum)

Kent officers, Faversham, 1899. (Courtesy of Kent Police Museum)

with committing a felony, the third party needing only to justify to the constable his reasonable grounds for any suspicions he might have.

Before investigating cases of alleged felonies, it was wise to give such situations careful consideration. Charges of felony often emanated from disorderly houses where unscrupulous parties might mislead a constable or lure him into a potentially hazardous situation. Far better to be accompanied by a colleague for back-up and as a witness.

During the day, the prevention of robberies was foremost of the constables' tasks, especially in towns where robbers, thieves and pickpockets easily merged into the crowds and carried out their depredations.

Where, despite a constable's vigilance, a robbery was discovered to have been committed, the message was to be passed to all neighbouring beats to be on the lookout for thieves. Instant searches of places where stolen property was suspected to be concealed could be implemented, although a search warrant was advised if it was thought the person concealing the property might be a bad or suspicious character.

Goods stolen during the night were often taken first thing the following morning to be pawned and a vigilant constable had every right to follow any suspect into a pawnbroker's shop to examine and arrest a felon.

A constable had the right to stop and search anyone he spotted carrying a parcel, particularly between dusk and dawn, if he believed that parcel might contain stolen items. This power was further defined for application in the countryside, as this extract, relating to the Poaching Prevention Act 1862, from the Surrey Constabulary's instruction book highlights:

> *The constable has power to search in any highway, street, or public place, any person whom he may have good cause to suspect of coming from any land where he shall have been unlawfully in search or pursuit of game, or any person aiding or abetting such persons, and having in his*

possession any game unlawfully obtained, or any gun, part of a gun, nets or engines used for killing or taking game; and also to stop and search any cart or conveyance in which the constable shall have good cause to suspect that any such game, or any such article or thing is being carried by any such person; and should there be found any game, or any such article or thing, as aforesaid, upon such person, cart or other conveyance, to seize and detain such game, article or thing. The word game is to include hares, rabbits, pheasants, partridge, woodcocks, snipes, black or moor game, as well as the eggs of these birds.

Before determining any felonious intention and making an arrest, he was to exercise great caution and discretion, judging the person's appearance and demeanour, the property he was carrying and any account he might give. This guidance was to ensure the great and good – who apparently had every right to be carrying parcels – were not wrongfully arrested. However, any man intent on felony was unlikely to welcome being stopped and searched, and therefore very likely to resist arrest. This may have been less of a problem in urban areas where a constable could summon help. But in rural, sparsely populated areas a constable risked serious assault, as PC Edward Atkinson discovered when he met a man carrying a suspicious-looking parcel on the Leeds and Wakefield turnpike at 2am on 1 March 1874. The fowl-thief resisted arrest by repeatedly kicking the constable so hard he spat blood. His extensive injuries included a very swollen black-eye, lacerated ears, wounds on the back of the head and bruises covering his ribs and hands.

The rules also defined certain malicious acts as felonies:

- Setting fire to any church or chapel or to any house, stable, coach house, outhouse, warehouse, office, shop, mill, malthouse, hop barn or granary, or any building used as a manufactory.

- Pulling down or destroying any public bridge with intent to render it impossible or dangerous.
- Throwing down any tollbar or fence belonging to any turnpike gate.
- Killing, maiming or wounding any cattle.
- Setting fire to any stack or crop of grain, straw, or hay.
- Cattle-, horse- and sheep-stealing.
- Receiving stolen goods, embezzlement.
- All cases of forging and coining.

Any offence that was not a felony was generally classed as a misdemeanour. This included riots, unlawful assembly, affrays and assaults. Attempts to commit felonies or misdemeanours were misdemeanours in themselves. A warrant was required to arrest anyone committing a misdemeanour, unless he had already been arrested and escaped.

There appears to have been another class of crime, which was neither defined as felony nor misdemeanour, but included the following for which any perpetrator could be arrested without a warrant:

- Stealing any animal or any bird or beast ordinarily kept in a state of confinement.
- Killing, wounding or taking any dove or pigeon.
- Stealing or culling, breaking, rooting up or destroying with intent to steal or damage, any tree or shrub.
- Stealing or cutting, breaking or throwing down with intent to steal or damage, any part of any fence or any wooden post, pale or rail used as a fence.
- Stealing, damaging or destroying any plant, fruit or vegetable production growing in any garden, orchard, nursery ground, hothouse, greenhouse or conservatory, or any cultivated fruit or plant used for the food of man or beast, or for medicine, or for distilling or for dyeing or for the course of any manufacturer and growing in any land, open or enclosed.
- Obtaining any money, goods or valuables secured by means of false pretences.

- Maliciously doing damage to any property.
- Riotous, violent, or indecent behaviour in any church or chapel, or in any churchyard, or burial ground.
- Desertion from the army, royal navy, or militia.

In practice, it would seem a constable could make an arrest – even for those offences deemed as misdemeanours – by asserting the person was about to commit a breach of the peace. However, this decision could be tricky for an inexperienced constable as he would need to judge whether the parties were merely using quarrelsome and insulting or abusive words, or whether if, without his intervention, the situation was likely to escalate into violent affray – at which point he could be faced with a serious problem.

Having determined an arrestable offence had taken or was about to take place, the constable could move in on his felon. Without using unnecessary force or more violence than required to secure the offender he was to convey him to the police station or lock-up. Any striking or ill-treatment of the prisoner once he had him in safe custody was punishable by suspension or dismissal. No more constables than absolutely necessary were allowed to accompany the arrested person, and once the prisoner had been booked into custody, the constable was not to hang about in the police station for a break, but to return to his beat in all convenient speed and immediately walk around it to check no further crimes were in progress.

Only prisoners known to be common thieves could be searched, and only for implements of housebreaking, although the officer was to guard against the prisoner dropping stolen property or money, thereby losing essential evidence. However, if the charge was one of murder or wounding with intent to commit bodily harm, the constable was advised to 'carefully examine the prisoner's hands, clothing, and any weapon in his possession, and likewise carefully inspect the place where the offence was said to have been committed'.[27]

Female prisoners were searched by a woman, either the wife of the police officer who resided at the station or another woman appointed to the role. Bradford appointed Mary Field, the wife of Inspector

Joseph Field, and when Mary passed away in 1852, the role was continued by their daughter Elizabeth at a salary of £5 per year (£555).

Where an arrest had been made only on suspicion the prisoner had committed a felony, the constable was to question the prisoner in the presence of a superior officer, usually a superintendent. If the person accused was being taken into custody on a third party's say-so, it was desirable for that third party to accompany constable and prisoner to the station, in order to substantiate the charge. Questions were posed to the accused about his address, place of work or if he had a father or mother. The constable was to follow this up before going to court the following morning so he could apprise the magistrate of the circumstances – especially if as a result of his enquiries the person he had arrested was found to be innocent.

Constables had detailed instructions for the correct questioning of those taken into custody, as this extract demonstrates:

> *With regard to the questioning of prisoners whilst in custody, it has been well observed that no practice has been more censurable and unjust, than that so common amongst officers of justice putting questions to persons in custody, with the view of obtaining answers that may afterwards be used in evidence against them. It should ever be borne in mind by the constable, that whilst it is his duty to do his utmost to prevent crime, it is no part of his province to 'make evidence'. It is at all times right that a person taken into custody should be informed of the charge against him; it is proper that the constable should listen to any statements which the prisoner may think it advisable to make, and to note down, and bear in remembrance all that he has said; but it is an abuse of power and authority in any constable to question an accused, and to draw from him statements which, in an unguarded moment, and in the confusion and embarrassment of his position, he may unadvisedly and*

incautiously make; and that, too, to interrogations not
themselves reduced to writing, perhaps equivocally put,
and the bearing and purport of which he may not
understand.[28]

The constable was to notice and, if possible, note down at the time
'every expression which may assist the ends of justice that he may be
prepared to repeat it when required'.

Any evidence obtained from a prisoner as a result of threats,
promises or inducements, however slight, made by the constable,
rendered such evidence inadmissible. However, any facts discovered
by following up the information so obtained could be later used in
evidence.

Prisoners locked up at the police station 'were not to be allowed
spirituous liquors, wine, beer, or tobacco, unless prescribed by a
medical man',[29] but could purchase other refreshments of their choice.

Those already rendered insensible through intoxication were to be
visited by a doctor when practicable and medical aid given to those
who required it. Others in custody were to be visited frequently by the
officer-in-charge and have means of communicating with that officer,
although they were not to be treated with any degree of familiarity,
even those already very well-known to the police.

A constable who had taken a person into custody was to appear
against him or her at the magistrates' court the next day, except where
doing so might put his personal safety at risk. The police officer was
expected to gather any of the witnesses to the court, which could
include, for example, the owner of any property stolen, the
pawnbroker who had accepted the goods to be pawned, and any other
witnesses to the crime. Everything the constable did was to be free
from bias and suspicion, which meant not going into a public house
with, or accepting drink from, witnesses or principals in any case.

As the prisoner before the magistrates was technically still in the
custody of the constable, and as 'nothing reflects greater disgrace on
a constable than the escape of a prisoner', he was to use every legal
precaution to prevent such escape. This might mean the constable

judging the accused appear in court handcuffed to him, to restrain him from acts of violence, potential escape or his rescue by friends.

Cases against suspects were to be stated clearly, candidly and succinctly, without embellishment. This might need prior preparation in order for the expected full and complete evidence to be stated. The evidence was to be delivered loudly and distinctly, and the constable was to stand in a respectful attitude. Nothing was to be held back whether for or against the accused, the constable having satisfied himself that every possible circumstance connected with the case had been thoroughly investigated. Hearsay evidence and that of one prisoner for or against another was not admissible, nor was circumstantial evidence. Once his evidence had been given, the constable was expected to remain silent and not butt in with additional evidence when other people were giving theirs.

Declarations by a person on the point of death, usually taken by an attending magistrate, were allowed as evidence against the accused, providing the person would have been a competent witness had he lived.

Constables appearing before the magistrates as prosecutors or witnesses were allowed daily payment to cover expenses, according to the distance they had to travel and for any overnight stay. Fare allowances were also made for those who had to travel by railway, and for those who travelled by other means a mileage allowance was paid. No constable was to be allowed money for railway fare not actually paid.

Cases sent for trial at the assizes or sessions generally incurred greater expense as the distances travelled were further. For example, in January 1848, Bradford's watch committee recommended a fixed allowance of 10 shillings a day (£55.50) for attending at Wakefield and 12 shillings for attendance at York (£66.60), plus a third class rail ticket for each prisoner. The allowance was to cover the day going and the day returning plus any overnight cost. Any extra days were paid at 6 shillings per day (£33.30).

Once given a custodial sentence or committed to trial at the assizes or sessions, prisoners were even more likely to try to make an escape and were therefore generally handcuffed to a constable while being conveyed from one place to another. The constable was cautioned against striking the prisoner unless in self-defence or vital to prevent his escape, and certainly not because the prisoner was 'merely violent in behaviour or language'.

Travelling a distance in each other's company occasionally gave prisoner and constable the opportunity to come to some chancy arrangements. It was recorded in Bradford's watch committee minutes of 13 August 1859:

> [T]he most objectionable practice has prevailed in the Police Office of allowing prisoners committed to Wakefield to give up money to the Police Constable conveying them to be afterwards delivered to the prisoners or some nominee of theirs, and also of allowing prisoners to go to public houses before being delivered to the House of Correction. Detective Shuttleworth has followed this improper practice in numerous instances but apparently with the knowledge of his superior officer, and the Chief Constable should be instructed to take measures for preventing the occurrence of such practices.

Police in Cheshire were also noted, contrary to orders, to walk prisoners distances up to 15 miles to gaol – pocketing the transport allowances for both prisoner and escort. Whether they called at a public house or not is not recorded.

Some forces quickly followed the Metropolitan Police's example and procured bespoke horse-drawn prison vans for both transporting rounded-up miscreants into custody and conveying convicted criminals to gaol, either directly or from the railway station. Horses and drivers were sometimes provided by a third party – Manchester's watch committee were informed that the city's Lamp, Scavenging and Hackney Coach Committee would provide horses and driver for the prison van at a cost of £126 per year in 1843 (£13,900).

Other forces were later in obtaining this form of transport – Bradford in 1878 and Birkenhead in 1879, for example – when tenders were invited for a prisoners' conveyance van divided into two compartments, each to hold up to six persons, and with a drivers' box for two constables and a covered seat at the back for a conductor.

Prison vans were not a failsafe way of ensuring prisoners arrived at their destination without incident.

A report from the *Manchester Courier and Lancashire General Advertiser* of 14 September 1880 describes an exciting scene when the horses pulling the Oldham prison van, taking its six captives to Strangeways Gaol in Manchester, set off in fright, the driver having alighted. Somehow the constable at the back managed to stay aboard, and by whistling and shouting as the vehicle careered down Cheetham Hill Road and along York Street, alerted other vehicles to get out of the way. As they hurtled into the crowded Corporation Street, it became more difficult for people to leap out of their path, and at the junction with Halliwell Street the van crashed into a lurry, knocking over the attached horse and causing one of the prison van horses to fall, badly lacerating its shoulder. The occupants of the prison van 'were considerably alarmed', but uninjured. The wounded horse was treated by a vet and replaced and the prisoners safely conveyed to their destination. The prison van was slightly damaged on one side.

In May 1895, a sensational suicide was reported to have taken place inside a prison van, after a man, sentenced to three months hard labour for breaking into a dwelling house, was transported from a police station to Derby Gaol. The man, George Duffield, apparently a surly character, was known by the local police sergeant as he had been a bailiff for around eighteen years, but had recently been out of work. Although he had the 'seedy appearance of someone who had been drinking the previous night', he seemed fine as he was put into one of the prison van's compartments. However, on arrival at Derby Gaol, he did not respond to the constable's request to get out of the van and remained sitting in the corner. The constable, hearing a dripping sound – Duffield's blood – discovered the prisoner had cut his own throat. He was removed, barely conscious, from the van. A doctor hastily attended, but Duffield expired inside the prison gates. At the inquest, the coroner found the prisoner had been thoroughly searched by a constable after visiting the 'closet', but had managed to conceal a razor somewhere about his person. A verdict of suicide whilst in a temporary fit of insanity was returned.

One perfectly innocent man experienced incarceration in a prison van – albeit without the company of ne'er do wells – but for a longer period than usually endured. An inquisitive young tradesman from Birmingham, who had cycled to Warwick Summer Quarter Sessions in 1891 to hear a case in which his friend was the prosecutor, finding himself with a little leisure time decided to inspect the prison van. As he was looking into one of the compartments, the door slammed and locked behind him. The chief warder was unable to leave his post in the dock to free the young man until proceedings were over, so he remained imprisoned for ninety minutes. His friends did their best to cheer him during this time, supplying him with brandy and soda through the ventilator. On his release, he vowed he would have nothing to do with a prison van ever again.

Prison vans were subjected to a great deal of wear and tear, therefore periodically needed replacing. In 1899, the chief constable of Birkenhead was again authorised to invite tenders for the construction of a new vehicle. It was to weigh 17 hundredweight (almost a ton) and be capable of carrying eleven prisoners. The existing conveyance had become old and dilapidated:

> *The prisoners are huddled together, male and female, vicious and unfortunate, clean and unclean. The blinds are pulled down in order to hide the prisoners from the public gaze but the back window is left open for the purpose of ventilation. The prisoners' friends who can see them through this necessary aperture shout remarks to them and are frequently answered in oaths and ribald language [...] On a recent occasion when returning from Walton the door of the omnibus fell off.*[30]

Carlisle Journal – Friday 12 April 1850

THE PRISON VAN.

'Tis night! The time for calm and sleep
But the din of the city is loud and deep;
In a thousand hearts the pulses swell
To the song, to the dance, to the bacchanal's yell
And night is the time, night is the time
For deeds of shame, and revel, and din –
For the crowning work of a life of sin,
O night is the time

The streets are fill'd, as at broad noon-day,
With rushing crowds of grave and gay;
Shout, and jeer, and whirl, and crash,
As countless vehicles onward dash.
But one – it is huge and grim, and black.
And hath no follower in its track,
Gloomily hurries on its course,
As though it were shunned by man and horse; –
'Tis the prison van!

Methinks I pierce the outward gloom
Of that moral pest – that living tomb
A boy is there, with head sunk low,
Whom virtue owned an hour ago;
A woman, whose wildly frantic prayer
Is mingled with curses of despair;
And one, grown old and grey in guilt,
Whose hand another's blood hath spilt; –
A haggard crowd!

But, could we see the souls within
That blighted mass of grief and sin;
The stern remorse from the aged wrung,

VICTORIAN POLICING

The penitent agony of the young;
The prayers that never reach the lips
In the blackness of the soul's eclipse
The shame, the fear, the terrible woe,
That only the wretched guilty know; –
Ah could we see!

Would we dare curse the vilest man
Who goes to death in that Prison Van?
Would we manacle, brand, transport or slay
Whom God has formed of the self-same clay?
O no! we would seek to cheer; to bless;
To minister to his dark distress;
Dispel the clouds that about him roll;
And burst the bonds that fetter his soul
In that Prison Van!

April 1850, J.P. Douglas

Chapter 8

The dangers of making an arrest

Being arrested and charged could mean a long period in custody without income, penal servitude, or worse. Transportation was still being practised until 1868 for a long list of offences, some relatively minor. After 1861, the death penalty was only imposed on felons who had committed murder, arson in the Royal Dockyards, treason or piracy, but there was possibly still a fear of being hanged since, until the Punishment by Death Act in 1832, crimes eligible for the death penalty had included theft, shoplifting and stealing sheep, cattle and horses, counterfeiting and forgery.

Little wonder most felons doggedly resisted arrest, causing the police to sustain a catalogue of assaults and injuries in the execution of their duties – even after the passing of the Offences Against the Person Act in 1861 (see Appendix 3).

The records of the West Riding Constabulary Force, with its area of duty covering both urban and rural areas, reveal wide and varied crimes and ways of assaulting the police to avoid arrest. Felons carried implements, which as well as being used in their nefarious activities were often brought into play against the police. Murderous and serious assaults on the police made exciting reading in the local newspapers and the descriptions of them were often graphic.

PC William Wallace was on duty in Boroughbridge in the small hours of 22 October 1870 when he spotted two men 'burglariously' attempting to enter the home of Joseph Stubbs, a spirit merchant. As PC Wallace tried to apprehend the men, they attacked him with the hedge slashers they were carrying, fracturing his arm in several places. They escaped, leaving behind a crowbar, spade and large mallet.

Although a reward was offered for their arrest it is not clear whether they were ever found.

Another victim of assault that prevented arrest was PS William Wilmot, who when on duty with another colleague at 1am came across three men, one of whom carried a gun. The police bravely asked the men why they were about at such an early hour, but were told to 'stand back'. One of the felons threw large cinders, striking PS Wilmot on the head, inflicting a severe wound. During the ensuing struggle the felons escaped.

One of the earliest serious assaults, committed shortly after the new constabulary force had been established, was upon PC Robert Walker, who had joined the force on Christmas Eve 1856. By 20 March 1857, he had lost three fingers. Newly stationed at Wombwell near Barnsley, where several robberies had been committed, the constable had been instructed to watch a field where several sheep were pastured. He saw three men come, select a sheep and slaughter it, before attempting to apprehend them. One was armed with a life preserver and a carving knife, but the constable, being a strong man, initially overpowered him, knocking the two others into a stream using the first man's life preserver. He was in the process of handcuffing the man when the sheep-stealers called four other men to their rescue. The gang set about beating and stabbing PC Walker in the head and neck, but he valiantly held on until one of the gang, seizing the knife used to slaughter the sheep, cut off two of the constable's fingers and left another hanging by a piece of skin. Still the constable fought on, striking his assailants so hard the stick he was using broke into several pieces. However, the unequal struggle meant he finally had to let go and, leaving him for dead, the men escaped. One was heard to say, 'There, we've killed the bugger.' Once he could move the constable managed to make his way to the house of a Mr Walton, who conveyed the blood-covered and exhausted man home. Word was despatched to the main police station in Barnsley and a surgeon was sent to tend to PC Walker's wounds. An inspection of the scene in daylight led to the grisly discovery of Walker's severed fingers and the weapons used in his attack.

Although the men initially escaped, a manhunt over the next few days succeeded in apprehending eight men, who were brought before PC Walker in his own bedroom (he being confined to bed through his injuries) for identification. Only one, Henry Waller, was recognised and the others discharged.

Henry Waller appeared at York Summer Assizes on 8 July 1857, charged with cutting and wounding PC Walker with intent to resist his lawful apprehension. Waller's defence argued it was a case of mistaken identity and he could not possibly have carried out the attack since he had recently been lamed in a fight. However, the jury quickly found him guilty when a previous case of felony against him was also proved. He was sentenced to fourteen years of penal servitude for his violent crime and was eventually transported to Australia on 30 September 1861 aboard the *Lincelles*.

At the end of the trial the judge awarded PC Walker the sum of 20 guineas (£2,331) for his gallant conduct and added that he hoped the county would give the constable a permanent situation in the police, the duties of which he would be able to perform as some compensation for the injuries he had sustained.

In the meantime, newspapers across the country reported:

> *It will be remembered that about three months ago a constable named Walker, one of the West Riding constabulary, had a very severe single-handed encounter with a number of sheep stealers at Wombwell. The officer narrowly escaped with his life, and amongst other severe injuries which he received, two or three of his fingers were cut off. To provide against such contingencies the new county constabulary force has a superannuation fund to fall back upon, but independent of this, the West Riding force, as mark of their approval of Walker's valour and conduct on the occasion referred to have got up a special subscription, amounting to £36, which they have just handed over to him. £6 of the amount was by his desire spent in the purchase of a neat silver watch, on which is*

105

engraved the following inscription: "Presented, with £30, to PC Walker by Colonel Cobbe and the members of the West Riding Constabulary, as a mark of their appreciation of his courage in the struggle with sheep stealers on the night of the 20th March, 1857, Wombwell." The farmers in the neighbourhood of Wombwell have also entered into a subscription, and presented him with the handsome sum of £33, and in addition, several magistrates and gentlemen residing near Doncaster, in highly complimentary terms forwarded to the same officer 15 guineas, thus making the total amount (exclusive of the watch) £78 15 shillings.

PC Walker did return to some kind of full duty after his recovery, as records show he was once again assaulted and injured – thrown down by Thomas Thistlethwaite when on duty on 22 June 1867, dislocating his right elbow and receiving other injuries. He finally retired with a daily pension of 2s 9d (£14) in April 1877.

Police officers who were in any fit physical state after a felon they were attempting to arrest had resisted so violently were obliged to give chase if that felon escaped. If necessary, they were to break open the doors of any house or other building wherein a felon might seek refuge, in order to re-arrest him. Even for a fit man giving chase was not without risk of injury. Constables had to jump over walls, climb iron railings, leap across streams, run along railway lines, roads and footpaths, and many broke or bruised limbs, ruptured themselves, caught their testicles, or just slipped, tripped and fell in pursuit of their quarry.

Poachers, fowl-stealers and pigeon-stealers seem to have been some of the main perpetrators of violent assaults against the police. Their chosen crime required them to carry guns, knives, clubs and so on with which to kill game, and these were regularly used to inflict serious wounds on any constable who tried to arrest them. Tackling poachers was not for the faint-hearted.

As a reaction to the huge increase in 'the Practice of going out by night for the purpose of destroying Game', which 'has in very many instances led to the commission of Murder, and of other grievous offences', the Night Poaching Act had been introduced in 1828 and enhanced in 1844 for the 'more effectual Prevention of Persons going armed by Night for the Destruction of Game'.

It empowered owners or occupiers of land, lords of manors, or their servants to apprehend offenders and deliver them into the custody of a peace officer, so they might appear before two justices of the peace.

The penalties increased with the number of repeat offences committed. First offenders were sentenced to three months with hard labour, a second offence was six months and hard labour, and a third offence could mean transportation for between seven and fourteen years. Offenders who violently resisted apprehension with any gun, crossbow, fire arms, bludgeon, stick, club or other offensive weapon, would be guilty of a misdemeanour and liable to either transportation or imprisonment, regardless of it being a first or second offence.

The Act seems to have had little impact on reducing poaching. Victorian newspapers regularly reported murderous or serious affrays between poachers and gamekeepers, often resulting in the death of one or other or both factions. For the poachers, it was more than just a way of feeding a family from the land and had become a conflict between the peasants and the landed gentry. One affray between two gamekeepers and seven poachers, which took place in November 1850 near Leamington on the estate of Lord Guernsey, was headlined in contrasting newspapers as either 'A Murderous Affray with Poachers' or 'Victory for the Poachers'. The latter describes with some elation that the desperate onslaught made by the poachers on 'his lordship's keepers' resulted in both keepers receiving 'frightful injuries, one of them being dreadfully shattered'. The keeper later died of the wounds inflicted on his scalp by a poacher brandishing a cutlass, but the report fails to mention that one of the poachers also died, shot by his own gun.

According to the book *The Long Affray* by Harry Hopkins, battles such as these resulted in the deaths of forty-two gamekeepers between

1833 and 1843 and the serious injuries of more than forty gamekeepers in Staffordshire in 1860–61.

The Poaching Prevention Act 1862 gave the constables additional powers to search persons, without warrant in certain cases, and to seize and detain any goods and to apply for a summons for the offender to appear before the magistrates.

When PS Barclay spotted three colliers from Castleford apparently stealing game in 'a very lonely place' on a November night in 1878, he had no chance to take evasive action before they started to pelt him with large stones and knocked him down with a large stick. Having beaten and kicked him till he lost consciousness, they made their escape. Recovering slightly, he managed to crawl to his home at the police station and was assisted into bed, needing a fortnight off work to recover from his ordeal. Already known to the police as notorious poachers, two of the men were ultimately apprehended and brought before the court. Although the prisoners had each been convicted several times previously under the Poaching Prevention Act (and for assaults on the police), they were only sentenced to six months' imprisonment.

As well as guns, bludgeons and cutlasses, the poacher had another weapon of attack – his dog. Thomas Fletcher from Linton near Wetherby was carrying a suspicious bundle under his arm when he met PC George Trafford, who asked him to reveal the bundle's contents. Fletcher refused, and as the constable grabbed the bag, Fletcher punched him in the face and urged his bull terrier dog to bite the constable's legs. A great tussle ensued with Fletcher goading his dog on. The policeman's young son, seeing his father being attacked, rushed in and bravely fended off the dog with a stout stick. Eventually, PC Trafford gained control, handcuffed the poacher and marched him off to Wetherby, where he appeared before magistrates and was committed to gaol for two months.

Understandably, some constables preferred to stay out of the way of poachers, instead observing them from a distance, gathering evidence and awaiting reinforcements. This was not without its own hazards, however, as the personnel records of two individuals demonstrate. Both PC William Widdop and PS Herbert Poyser sustained severe leg injuries merely watching notorious poachers, the former by falling through a roof, the latter climbing a wall to get a better view.

By the end of Queen Victoria's long reign, the newspapers were still full of reports of gangs of poachers carrying out violent acts, so little was achieved in the prevention of the crime. But perhaps the brave actions of the police meant higher numbers of poachers were brought to justice.

Another formidable duty in which the police were likely to receive injury was that of dispersing prize-fights. Often attended by crowds and with large sums of money at stake, violence was not confined to the pugilists' ring.

A constable was advised not to attempt to prevent a fight taking place without assistance, but in receiving information of an intended prize-fight, or seeing crowds of disorderly people heading towards a place where a fight might be in progress, was to pass word quickly to the chief constable in order for sufficient forces of policemen to be gathered to disperse the combatants.

Scouts posted to look out for police presence meant fights might be delayed until the police had receded, only to start up in another location.

One such fight in Long Eaton near Nottingham, due to take place in nearby meadows, was initially prevented by the police, but later recommenced with fatal consequences. That the fight was extremely violent is evident from the newspaper report of June 1850 in which it describes the fight lasting for seventy-five minutes until James Brown, aged 22, lay upon the turf, freely vomiting blood. He was hastily conveyed to a railway carriage by his backers, but died before the train reached Nottingham. On hearing of Brown's death, his antagonist Richard Hall, aged only 17, instantly decamped along with his backers and associates. He was later arrested and tried at Nottingham Assizes on 23 July. His sentence, for manslaughter, was a mere month's imprisonment.

Only a few weeks later there was another fatal prize-fight, this time in Frimley near Bagshot in Surrey. Described by the press as 'an old professor of the science of pugilism', William Gill terminated the contest after fifty-three rounds by landing a fearful blow on Thomas Griffiths, 'an aspirant for pugilistic honours'. A special train from London had brought the combatants and their followers to Frimley and the battle money was understood to be the huge sum of £200 (£22,200). Griffiths died of his injuries and Gill and the crowd once again dispersed without any arrests being made.

Somehow, despite the crowds, attendant noise, and length exceeding an hour, many fights passed off wholly without interference from the police. Fast and furious, and with neither party willing to concede defeat, fights often ended up with both men 'severely punished' and in need of attention. One can only imagine the state of the two men in Manchester who, having fought thirty rounds in an hour, had to be bathed in an adjacent canal before they could be taken home.

One prize-fight that did not pass without police interference was that which took place in the wild and lonely moors bordering Yorkshire, Derbyshire and Cheshire on 11 February 1868.

The stakes of the fight between George Potts, alias Patsey, of Sheffield, and James Larvin of Dewsbury, were high at £25 a head (£2,775), and on receiving word that a prize-fight was to take place, the superintendent of the Huddersfield division of the West Riding Constabulary instructed a search to be made of the houses of Holmfirth on 10 February. As nothing was uncovered, the following night the 'low beerhouses' were searched for prize-fighters. Word came that the fight was to take place near Saltersbrook on the old turnpike road that later became the Woodhead Pass. Arriving at the Junction Inn, the police found a boxing ring already in place and a crowd of between 600 and 1,000 people awaiting the combatants. The fight was prevented but the determined mob, with around twenty police following, headed off over the moors towards Cheshire to recommence the fight in another county. On reaching the border, the mob found a contingent of Cheshire police prepared to prevent the fight:

The ruffians, perceiving the straits into which they had thrown themselves, returned and charged the Yorkshire officers. A desperate affray ensued, in which the police, being the weakest party in point of numbers, not exceeding twenty men, were worsted. Volleys of stones and other missiles were showered upon the constables, who had to beat a retreat, several of the men being rendered hors de combat. *Inspector Nunn received a severe scalp wound; Sergeant Turner had two or three of his ribs fractured, and now lies in a dangerous state; the head of PC Harwood was frightfully lacerated; Constable Atkinson, of Holmfirth, was also injured in the struggle; and a constable from the Barnsley division of police was also hurt. Potts, one of the combatants, has been apprehended by the Cheshire Constabulary, and it is expected others who participated in the attack upon the officers will shortly be in custody.* (*Huddersfield Chronicle,* 15 February 1868)

Fifteen men were eventually brought before the magistrates, five charged with assaulting the police and ten with aiding and abetting the assault. The defence barrister stated that not only was it necessary for the police to prove a breach of the peace had taken or was about to take place, but they must also prove it was their duty to be there. To make the stone-throwing an offence, it had to be shown it had been done while the police were doing something that the law said they had the right to do.

Eventually, the magistrates decided to send those charged with assault to the Wakefield Spring Sessions for trial and those who had aided and abetted were dismissed.

On 6 April 1868, four people – Benjamin Chappell (a miner from Silkstone), Thomas Ibberson (a 'respectable' butcher from Huddersfield), William Marsden and Matthew Milnes – were each fined £10 (£1,110) and asked to enter into a requirement of £25 (£2,770) to keep the peace for twelve months, or on default be imprisoned for six months.

Assaults on police continued to be a major problem. They deterred suitable men from joining the police force, caused many experienced and trained men to leave, and occasioned men to take sick leave to recover from injury.

When the Habitual Criminals Act was passed in 1869, as well as its main objectives of the supervision of criminals and a proper registration system to enable the recognition of repeat offenders when brought to trial, one of its principal provisions was to impose more severe punishments for assaults on the police. At the time the penalty of one month's imprisonment or a fine of £5 (£555) for assaulting a police officer was less than the penalty for common assault. The new Act allowed sentences of six months, with or without hard labour, to be fixed.

In 1870, when James Withers, the then head constable of the recently established Huddersfield Borough Force, submitted his annual report on the borough's crime statistics, he noted the hoped-for reduction in assaults on police since the new Act had not materialised, and the number committed to gaol or fined had increased from twenty-six to thirty-two persons. His expectations were not realised until 1872, when the number of assaults was a mere twenty. This turned out to be a blip as, in 1873, the number was back to thirty-three, from whence it continued to rise, reaching forty in 1876.

Whether the justices accepted that assaults on police were a serious offence is debatable, as the sentencing seems to fall far short of what was prescribed in the 1869 Act.

Two serious assaults that took place almost twenty-five years apart show inconsistencies in the penalties given, even though both trials took place in Yorkshire.

The first, in February 1872, related to a serious assault on PC Benjamin Grayson by Bradley Newton at a scattered location known as Clough Head near Golcar, where the constable was inspecting the public houses. At the beginning of the trial the superintendent conducting the case alluded to the injuries received by PC Grayson, and that if the case was proved, a pecuniary penalty would not be sufficient punishment for such a gross and unprovoked attack on the police. He voiced that the accused should be imprisoned for up to six months.

During the trial, the bench heard from several witnesses how Newton came up to PC Grayson and shoved him in the chest into the middle of the road. The constable retaliated and, shaking Newton by his coat collar, threatened to report him. Newton offered his hand and asked the constable to forgive him this time, but when the constable rejected this, Newton, grabbing him by the belt, told the constable: 'I'll give you something to report me for then,' and started kicking Grayson in the legs, throwing him to the ground.

The constable was kicked in the head, face and other parts of the body until, having lost a good deal of blood, he became sick and faint and was carried home.

Some witnesses deposed the fight had been a fair one between two men, but another heard the constable cry out, 'Is a man to be killed; will no-one help me?' (*Huddersfield Chronicle*, 17 February 1872).

The manner of Bradley Newton's arrest was alluded to by his defence, he being dragged out of bed by three policemen, handcuffed, and forced to dress (with them on), then beaten with a truncheon, taken to Huddersfield, and locked up in the cell from Sunday night until Tuesday without warrant or bail. The defence concluded that the prisoner could not be charged with murder, had it ensued, because of the illegality of his apprehension.

However, having heard various witnesses, many of them friends of the accused, the bench deliberated for only a few minutes before the chairman stated:

> We believe the evidence of the policeman is true, that there was an assault made upon him by the defendant, and whatever the witnesses say, the evidence of Dr Webster (police surgeon) goes to show he was used in an aggravated way. If policemen, when on duty, are to be assaulted by rough men like Bradley Newton, and surrounded by other men, who will not render the officer

*any assistance, there would be no safety for them. The
magistrates will, when policemen do their duty properly,
especially where their conduct is unexceptionable, like
that of Grayson, protect them in the discharge of that duty
to the full extent of their power. (Huddersfield Chronicle,
17 February 1872)*

Bradley Newton was sent to prison for three months with hard labour.
PC Grayson recovered and went back to his duties. His good and
steady policing, cited in the trial, continued and he was promoted
through the ranks, becoming superintendent in April 1887.

The second incident, in 1895, was an assault so serious the
policeman died from peritonitis, caused by inflammation and gangrene
of the small intestine, eleven days after the attack.

The brutal assault on PS Winpenny took place in Liversedge, West
Yorkshire, late at night on Saturday 23 November 1895, when the
sergeant attempted to arrest a drunk and disorderly woman, Ruth
Colbeck, who had refused to give her name when asked. Ruth threw
herself to the floor, dragging Winpenny with her, biting his finger and
screaming 'murder!'. Her cries attracted a mob of around a hundred
or so rough men, who viciously attacked the policeman. Nine men
were subsequently arrested at their homes and conveyed to Dewsbury
where they and Colbeck appeared before the magistrates. The
newspapers described one man, Thomas Albert Heaton, currier, as
belonging to one of the best-known families in Liversedge, while the
others belonged to 'the labouring classes'.

At the time of the initial court hearing, when each mob member
was charged with inflicting grievous bodily harm on the sergeant,
Winpenny was still alive, but his life was despaired of and a dying
declaration had been taken by the deputy clerk to the court. Four of
the men, including Heaton, protested their innocence. All were
remanded in custody for a few days, but only Ruth Colbeck and
Benjamin Moorhouse appeared at the January Sessions in Leeds Town
Hall, charged on seven counts with assaulting Sergeant Wimpenny,
obstructing and resisting him in the execution of his duty.

Colbeck conducted her own defence, admitting she had been drunk but claiming the sergeant had assaulted her, trying to throttle her and knocking her about until she was bruised all over, when all she wanted to do was go home to her old father. Moorhouse, it was alleged, had come to her aid.

Other witnesses claimed the sergeant was beside himself with excitement and probably intoxicated.

The chairman told the jury there was no evidence to support the claims about Winpenny, but although death had been caused by a riotous crowd the two people here were not those who were accused of that offence.

Both prisoners were found guilty of the assault upon the officer while in the execution of his duty, Moorhouse being guilty of only a 'technical assault'. Although it was stated an assault against the police, whether a blow or a push, was assault against the law, both Colbeck and Moorhouse were sent to gaol for only a month.

Sergeant Winpenny was aged 50, and left a widow and eleven children, five of whom were 'too young to work'. His widow was granted a pension of £15 a year (£1,665) 'whilst she remained a widow' and an extra pension of £2 10s 0d a year (£277) for each of the youngest five children. The total was less than a third of her husband's salary. She never remarried.

'Murderous' was a frequently used adjective in the headlines and newspaper reports describing assaults on police. Although many men just got carried away in the excitement of an alcohol-fuelled, frenzied onslaught, some of the men committing these attacks did intend to kill their victims.

One small handwritten entry in the police records of Superintendent Thomas Birkill simply states: 'Murdered. He was deliberately shot at 7.30am and died 3 hours afterwards at Otley on 24th November 1887, by a poacher named William Taylor who had recently murdered his own child by shooting it for which crime the superintendent was endeavouring to apprehend him.'[31]

The newspapers gave a much fuller account of the:

*[...] reckless brutality and cruel determination that marked the tragedy when the people of Otley were thrown into a state of the wildest excitement by the too true report that a man resident in the town had, in attempting to shoot his wife, taken away the life of his child but ten weeks old, and afterwards, in his defiance of the police to arrest him, shot at and fatally wounded a superintendent of police, Mr Birkill. (*Yorkshire Post* and *Leeds Intelligencer*, 25 November 1887)*

The 'author of the ghastly outrage', William Taylor, had formerly been a farmer with his father, but had thrown away his opportunities, given way to drink and 'resorted to the adventurous pastime of poaching', before being finally disowned by his family. He had worked occasionally for a joiner, but generally spent time in idle pursuits while his wife tried to earn a living as a char. He had lately managed to escape the clutches of the police, but had been twice convicted of being drunk and riotous in 1877 and had also been fined 10 shillings (£55.50) for game trespass in 1879.

The evidence brought before the magistrates told how Taylor's wife was trying to comfort their baby daughter, who had bronchitis, in the middle of the night. The fire would not draw so she had opened the cottage door to create a draught. Slamming the door closed, Taylor grabbed his double-barrelled gun and shouted he would make the fire burn by shooting at the chimney. Fearful of his uncontrollable temper, and as he was making violent threats, his wife rushed out of the cottage and into the yard, still clutching the baby. Taylor fired the gun at his wife but missed, instead shooting the baby in her back.

Unaware of the baby's injury, Mrs Taylor sought refuge with a neighbour who noticed blood seeping through the shawl. A doctor was called but could not save the baby's life.

Ellis Brumfitt Hartley, who lodged with the Taylors, had managed to escape from the house before Taylor could shoot him, and raised the alarm with two police constables. They and two sergeants approached the house, but by this time Taylor had locked himself and his other daughter in the building. Not wishing to endanger the child's life, the police attempted to negotiate with Taylor, but all suggestions of capitulation were received with contempt, even the entreaties of his own brother. This defiance continued for hours, but when it became known the baby had died and the charges were now more serious, Superintendent Birkill was sent for.

By now a large crowd had gathered to watch the proceedings. While the two sergeants guarded the back door of the cottage, Birkill and the two constables attempted to break open the other door with a crowbar. Failing to heed the precautions he had earlier given to his subordinates, Birkill came within sight of Taylor, who shot him from an open window. Fatally wounded, Birkill fell backwards into the arms of PC Wildman and, although attended by a doctor and two surgeons, never regained consciousness.

In the meantime, attempts to capture Taylor continued. Inspector Crow attended from Ilkley and additional constables quietly staked-out the cottage. Presuming the police had left, and needing coal for the fire, Taylor eventually emerged from the cottage carrying a shovel and a carving knife. As soon as he peered around the door, he was grabbed by PC McDonald and held by other officers. Although entrapped, he still managed to deal McDonald a nasty blow on the face with his shovel. The crowd, now numbering several hundred, seeing Taylor in chains, shouted curses and asserted that if they had their way he would pay the penalty without the formality of a trial. He called out to the crowd he didn't give a damn and he had now got his revenge.

Charged with the murder of his child and Superintendent Birkill, Taylor merely remarked callously, 'It's all very well for you to say that; but it's all my eye and Peggy Martin.'

When called as a witness by the magistrates, Ellis Hartley, the lodger, told that Taylor had almost died aged 20, when he was badly beaten about the head at Timble near Otley. Since that time, he had suffered with epilepsy and other fits, especially when he had been tipsy. Prior to the epileptic fits, he would be in low spirits and refuse to eat, and have a 'queer and wild look about his eyes'. Taylor had been frequently known to search the floor for things that were not there, and in the same way had been known to turn the carpets. Hartley related how he sometimes heard the prisoner whistle, sing and pray all night. These things usually occurred two or three days after he had been drinking. A few days before the murders, Mrs Taylor had called Hartley to observe her sober husband trying to put his legs through the sleeves of his coat, under the impression he had got hold of his trousers. The following day Taylor's eyes were rolling about, he was nervously rubbing his hands and trembling all over.

However, there was clear evidence of Taylor's murderous intent – the reloaded shotgun and the dozen cartridges found in his trouser pockets when arrested.

At the subsequent trial at Leeds Assizes in February 1888, Taylor's sanity was questioned before proceedings began. Although two doctors, a solicitor and a vicar gave their opinions that Taylor suffered from delusions and was therefore not of sound enough mind to stand trial, other medical witnesses opined that he knew right from wrong. Therefore, the trial went ahead. The grand jury returned a bill of indictment for murder but stated 'the accused was guilty of the act but was insane so as not to be responsible, according to law, for his actions at the time of the act and ordered to be detained during her Majesty's pleasure'.[32]

Taylor spent a few days in Armley Gaol in Leeds before being transferred to Broadmoor Lunatic Asylum.

About eight months after his committal, a newspaper report recorded a sad sequel to the story. Left alone in his cell at Broadmoor, Taylor, in a fit of maniacal insanity and delusion, managed to gouge out his own eyes with his fingers, causing him to lose his sight. In a letter dictated by him to his wife he pleaded: 'I should be very pleased for you to come and see me. It would not take you long to come. Old Satan told me to pull my eyes out, and I cannot see anything now. I have nothing else to tell you. From your affectionate husband, W. Taylor.' (*Leeds Times*, 7 September 1889)

Chapter 9

Crowd-control

Keeping order in the streets and other public places involved controlling crowds of either people making a statement (and therefore usually intending to cause trouble), or people participating in a public event (who might unwittingly cause trouble). Whatever the crowd's intention, the police were always outnumbered.

One of the earliest crowd-control duties for the Bradford borough police force was during Chartist outbreaks in the summer of 1848. The working-class movement originally emerged in 1836, seeking to gain political rights, including votes for all men over 21. By 1848, it had already presented two petitions to Parliament, with 1.2 million signatures in 1839 and 3.3 million in 1842. Both had been rejected. What became Chartism's final major push started after a third petition presented in April 1848 was also rejected, with marches and demonstrations taking place nationwide throughout that summer. Bradford was one of Chartism's strongholds.

In late May, the police arrested two of the leaders in Bingley on a charge of instructing marching exercises with Chartist national guards. They were committed to York Castle to await trial at the next assizes, but escaped when the two constables attempting to convey their prisoners to the railway station were surrounded by a vast crowd and attacked and beaten.

The following Sunday, a huge gathering of Chartists met at Wilsden, a village midway between Bradford, Bingley, Halifax and Keighley. Two to three thousand men, armed with bludgeons and preceded by others carrying black banners with pike heads, openly practised military marching before commencing their meeting during a massive thunderstorm. Agreeing to use arms to resist any attempts to capture their leaders, they also determined to further arm themselves cheaply by disarming the infantry who had been brought into Bradford, and taking the dragoons' horses. Although no riot took place, 'a great deal of treasonable and seditious language was employed by the various speakers', before the crowds marched back to their respective towns.

Expecting trouble, Bradford's authorities had sworn in an additional 2,000 special constables (chiefly merchants, manufacturers and tradesmen) and armed the police with cutlasses. Anticipating the police might need military support, two companies of the 39th Regiment of Foot, two troops of the 5th Dragoon Guards, and about thirty Horse Artillery, with two field pieces, arrived from Leeds. A further two infantry companies were ordered from Hull, the West Yorkshire Yeomanry were called out and the Yorkshire Hussars marched to advantageous points.

The newspapers carried the headline 'The Excited State of Bradford', describing the events that took place the next day, Monday 29 May 1848, when at 9am, Superintendent Brigg set out at the head of 100 specials with the goal of arresting Chartist leaders – particularly the notorious blacksmith and pike maker Isaac Jefferson, also known as 'Wat Tyler' – residing in the Manchester Road neighbourhood.

The mission was a brave one as the residents were known to be desperate, violent men who spoke loudly of tyranny and injustice. Finding Wat Tyler had made himself scarce when in danger of being arrested, the police were about to return when they were attacked by a mob who had followed them. Stones and brickbats were hurled, many of the specials had their staves snatched from their grasp and were beaten with them on their heads and backs. Even the women threw stones. Severely bruised and battered, the police made a hasty retreat towards Bradford Court House, chased by a braying mob.

By now the court house was strongly garrisoned with troops from the 5th Dragoon Guards, an infantry detachment and the yeomanry. Shops in the town had closed and put up their shutters. Inside the court house, military officers and magistrates devised a plan of operation.

At noon, a notice was issued strictly forbidding anyone to attend, take part in, or be present at the highly criminal and illegal practices of processions, drilling and military movements. All well-disposed people were urged to aid law enforcement and protect the public peace.

In a further bid to arrest Chartist leaders, Colonel Tempest announced the magistrates had decided a procession would revisit the neighbourhood where the riotous proceedings had occurred that morning. More troops had been called in from Colne and Manchester, and soldiers in the town now numbered around 800.

The police, carrying cutlasses, would lead the procession to Manchester Road, followed by the specials eight- or ten-abreast. Behind them would be a body of infantry and cavalry to protect the police if needed. The colonel bade the police to seize every Chartist leader and arrest anyone offering violence or obstructing their course.

At about 4pm, around 500 men assembled in front of the court house, each in their files and under the command of their various captains. Accompanying them on horseback were the mayor and four magistrates giving orders, advice and assistance.

The forces marched out of town and had barely arrived outside Wat Tyler's house when they were once again pelted with a volley of stones and brickbats. Two of the specials were so severely wounded they had to be removed. Others sustained less serious injuries. A pistol was fired into the air.

As the specials, their ranks now broken, bore down on the belligerent mob, the cavalry entered the fray and chased the crowd up the road. This gave the constables opportunity to scour the neighbouring streets, and many arrests were made. Notable was the arrest of Mary Mortimer, an 'Amazonian of the purest breed', who had been exceedingly violent and had 'tossed stones with the greatest intrepidity and fierceness, swore like a trooper, and declared she was a Chartist and would die a Chartist'. Her progress was only impeded by a dragoon, who thrust his sword across her path and into a wall. In contrast to this large, noisy woman was a little Irishman named Down who, brandishing a red-hot soldering iron, stoutly but unsuccessfully resisted arrest. Seventeen arrests were made, including a well-known

121

Chartist drill-master, William Sagar – but not Wat Tyler, who had once again apparently marched off as soon as the police came in sight.

The constables continued their searches of the now totally deserted Chartists' houses, finding in one an 8-foot-long staff topped with a pike, several cudgels and an old iron pan containing warm lead – recently used for making bullets.

But finding little further trace of Chartists or pikes in their 'poverty-stricken, dirty, wretched abodes', the procession returned to Bradford at around 6pm.

As a precaution against the trouble that might return to the streets, 100 or so specials were asked to patrol with the police for that and subsequent nights. At 6pm, officers were despatched to order publicans and beerhouse keepers to close their doors at 8pm, and at 6.30pm, the mayor, standing in front of the court house, read the Riot Act, in order to give the magistrates the power to clear the streets and public houses if necessary.

Fresh troops were brought into the court house for the night, but by 11pm, the streets were silent, punctuated at intervals by only the quick and regular step of patrols of specials and police as they marched through their beats.

The following day, 'the town was as quiet and calm as the weather was brilliant and beautiful'. Although soldiers still occupied parts of the court house, tranquillity continued the whole day.

Bradford's magistrates were not happy with the way the police had handled the Chartist uprising. On 21 June, the watch committee called a special meeting, after a letter from Mr Pollard dramatically asserted 'the magistrates have been thrown on their backs and thwarted in their measures by the police, some of whom have given information to the Chartists who had rendered themselves obnoxious to the police authorities, and the sooner they (the police) are done away with and the expense saved to the Corporation, the better'.[33]

The watch committee, feeling it should make 'the amplest investigation into these grave charges', requested to be furnished with the information on which the statements had been made with least possible delay, 'in order that the Watch Committee may proceed to deal with the cases in such a manner as to secure utmost integrity and efficiency in the Borough Police Force'.

Ten days later, Mr Pollard's reply to this request was discussed and found unsatisfactory. Again, the committee asked for distinctive and direct proof of his statements. None was forthcoming and so, on 15 July, the watch committee agreed to support the chief constable's view that police conduct during the Chartist riots had been exemplary, and informed Mr Pollard of the resolution.

The search for Wat Tyler and his cohorts continued for months, until Tyler was eventually apprehended by Superintendent Ingham at Swilling Hill, a small settlement between Halifax and Bradford, at 2.30am on 13 September 1848. Tired of life on the run, Wat Tyler quietly gave himself up. He was sentenced to four months in York Castle on 19 December for unlawfully drilling men on a moor 5 miles from Bradford on 28 May.

As the Chartist movement started its decline, a group of men called the Young Irelanders were becoming increasingly dissatisfied with the handling of the Great Potato Famine, denouncing the British government for doing too little to prevent so many Irish deaths. Inspired by revolutions in Europe, they led a small rebellion in protest against British rule. In July 1848, there was a stand-off between the police and the rebels at Ballingarry, County Tipperary, when forty-seven policemen barricaded themselves into a farmhouse. A gun battle ensued, and one of the rebels was fatally wounded. Realising they were likely to be outnumbered, the rebels eventually retreated.

Two of the leaders escaped to France: John O'Mahony, who later emigrated to America and founded the Fenian Brotherhood, and James Stephens who. having returned to Dublin, founded its Irish counterpart – the Irish Republican Brotherhood – in 1858.

As Fenianism grew it developed strong support in the north-west of England, particularly in Liverpool and Manchester where many Irish migrants had settled.

On 14 September 1867, the *Manchester Times* reported two men, said to be American-Irish, had been arrested under the Vagrancy Act.

They had been spotted in Swan Street in the small hours of 11 September by two vigilant constables who, because the men were unknown and were acting suspiciously, had followed them and taken them into custody. Two other men in the party had escaped. The pair who were arrested had offered considerable resistance and seemed desperate to get their hands into their pockets. The reason for this became clear when they were searched as each was found to be carrying a revolver loaded with gunpowder and a ball, and capped. They claimed they were American citizens, living on their own means and not on the streets for felonious purposes. However, Superintendent Maybury, certain he could connect them to the Fenian movement, asked they be remanded in custody, which was accordingly granted.

Maybury sent for a man from the Dublin police force to visit Manchester to identify the prisoners. One was identified as Colonel Thomas J Kelly, a key ally of James Stephens, the other as Captain Deasey.

On Wednesday 18 September, the men now known to be notorious Fenians were once again remanded pending further investigation and, after the day's court business had finished, were to be transported from the police cells to Belle Vue Gaol on Hyde Road, Manchester. Accompanying them in the prison van were three other prisoners who had been committed at the sessions, and Sergeant Brett, whose duty it had been for the previous twenty years to see all prisoners conveyed to the borough gaol. Although one of the magistrates had opined the officers in charge of the prison van ought to be armed on this occasion, the only precaution taken was to place a few policemen into a cart to follow the van. At around 3.30pm, the van left the city court and proceeded without incident until about halfway along the Hyde Road. As it passed under the railway bridge, it was ambushed by thirty to forty Irishmen firing shots at the driver, horses and prison van. The scene of indescribable mayhem seemed to paralyse the attending constables as two ambushers jumped onto the van roof and attempted to smash their way in with large stones, while others used picks, hammers and axes to break into the van by the door. Local men bravely came to the aid of the police, though it being a peaceable neighbourhood none had firearms. One of them was shot through his heel by one of the ambushers.

In the meantime, the men on the roof had broken through and a large stone struck Sergeant Brett on the head. A bullet was fired through the keyhole of the van door and, between the efforts of the prisoners inside and the mob outside, the door was opened. Brett was pushed and rolled out of the van. He had been shot through the temple and had one eye forced out of its socket. Although he was placed in a cab and rushed to the infirmary where his injuries were immediately attended to, he died at 5.30pm.

The mob and prisoners made their escape pursued by police, civilians and some railway workers. Despite a reward of £300 (£33,300), Kelly and Deasey were never recaptured, but twenty-six men were eventually arrested and brought to trial at Manchester Assizes on 26 September, all accused of murdering Sergeant Brett. Two men were acquitted and discharged and a further twelve discharged when no evidence was offered by the crown. Of the remaining dozen, seven were found guilty of riot and the misdemeanour of assaulting police officers whilst in the execution of their duty, being sentenced to five years' penal servitude. The other five were sentenced to death, but only three, William Gould (alias O'Brien), Michael Larkin and William Allen, were hanged for having 'feloniously, wilfully and with malice aforethought, killed and murdered Sergeant Brett'. A further two men were later arrested and tried, four months after the original trial. One was sentenced to death but escaped the hangman's noose through ill-health and died in prison about six months after his conviction.

The hanged men were hailed as martyrs by the Fenian movement. Fearful there might be continuing reprisals in a city that seemed to have become an epicentre for the resistance to British rule in Ireland, new police stations in Manchester were constructed with a cavity wall of steel between the brick interior and exterior walls to provide protection from gunpowder explosions.

Bradford also had a high proportion of Irish immigrants and, in September 1867, the Home Office thought it prudent to issue the force with twenty-four Colt revolvers and 1,000 rounds of ammunition in order that the police might be prepared. The watch committee ordered such arms could only be brought into force when the police were engaged in a service of danger and only entrusted to men of proven discretion, to be used in self-defence or resisting an attack made with a murdering weapon.

Other towns were also fearful of Fenian uprisings. In January 1868, calls came for volunteers to be sworn in as special constables as newspapers reported potential Fenian disturbances in Ripon, Merthyr Tydfil, Liverpool and Birkenhead. Within days 4,400 men were enrolled in Hull and 3,000 in Bradford. One surprise recruit to the Bradford special force was Isaac Jefferson:

> *Since his days in York Gaol, experience and suffering have greatly modified the early political views of Jefferson, and the Queen has not a more loyal and devoted subject than he in all her wide dominions. Though time has left slight marks of decay on his frame, he is yet a man of a fine portly form, with long flowing red beard. As he offered his name of "Isaac Jefferson" to the magistrates, previous to its being entered in the book, he added, as if to remind them of his former fame or notoriety, "better known as Wat Tyler," a remark which excited the smiles of the magistrates, who till that moment seemed unconscious of the importance of the personage who stood before them. "One man in his time plays many parts!" (Bradford Observer, 9 January 1868)*

A genuine fear of Fenian plots to blow up buildings pervaded the country in 1868. A cask of powder discovered by a passer-by near the railway works at Milford Haven caused the authorities to swear in several special constables, placing them at different points to guard against a suspected Fenian attack. On inquiry it was found the powder had been purchased for blasting at the railway works, but had arrived too late to be taken into storage.

Another report of a planned Fenian attack – on York Minster – led to the minster being specially guarded by troops and lit-up through the night, until it was discovered it was a 'miserable hoax' by a mischievous drunk who had sent a telegram, suggesting troops should be on standby to prevent an attempt to blow up the building.

There was also an alleged plot to blow up Shrewsbury Railway Station, reported in several newspapers:

> *Information was received on Saturday night of a Fenian plot, to blow up Shrewsbury railway station. The railway authorities immediately had the sewers blocked, and the station was watched all night. As might have been expected, nothing occurred.*

Rioting at elections had long been a common occurrence, as without a vote it seemed the only way the working classes might make their voices heard sufficiently to influence the election's outcome.

The 1867 Reform Bill became law on 15 August, pushed through by a minority Conservative government. By giving the vote to all male householders living in a borough constituency, lodgers who paid annual rents of at least £10 (£1,110), landowners with a rental income of £5 a year or more (£555), and tenants paying annual rents of at least £12 (£1,332), the electorate increased by around 1.5 million – almost doubling the previous size.

Being the first General Election since the passing of the Reform Bill, the 1868 election was unique, the 2,333,251 votes cast almost trebling that of the previous election in 1865. It is impossible to tell whether all these additional votes came from newly enfranchised voters, but it was certainly a less lack-lustre contest than its predecessor.

However, millions of working men, who did not own their own homes nor pay enough rent to qualify for a vote, were still left without a voice. Angry about this, they attacked polling stations and intimidated voters to disrupt the voting process.

Serious riots broke out in many towns and cities over the days in late November when polling took place. An account in the *Cork*

Examiner of 28 November 1868 related the news of riots in England and Wales, but barely mentioned the serious rioting that had also taken place in many Irish towns:

> *SERIOUS ELECTION RIOTS IN ENGLAND; LOSS OF LIFE. Some serious election riots resulted from the excitement of the elections yesterday. At Bolton some severe fights took place between English and Irish portions of the population. Many persons were injured, and considerable damage was done to property. Order was not restored until a company of soldiers arrived from Bury, and the Riot Act was read.*
>
> *At Wakefield, the disturbances which arose out of the nominations was of such serious character the military had to be sent for from Leeds. At the Wednesbury election, voters at Tipton were stoned by the roughs supporting Kenealy. Mr Joseph, surgeon, was cut on the head. A special constable who interfered and struck down the assailant was attacked. He took refuge in a house, but was dragged out, beaten with pick handles, and left for dead. His brother, a powerful fellow, was similarly hurt. The rioters attacked public houses and broke windows. Thirty policemen marched out and disarmed the rioters, who threatened a renewal of disturbances during the night. A company of rifles are under arms in Wolverhampton waiting orders from Tipton.*
>
> *There has been a serious riot in Newport. The military were called out, and charged the mob repeatedly. One person was killed, and several dangerously wounded. The town is now quiet.*

Barnsley in the West Riding of Yorkshire also saw serious rioting on 24 November. According to the police records, around forty-three constables from the West Riding Constabulary, called in to quell the disturbance, received injuries that night:

The disturbance reported yesterday was continued to a late hour Tuesday night and resulted in large number of persons being injured. The police needed their night lights, which illuminated the streets, and enabled them to clear the thoroughfares of the roughs, who in return fired large volleys of brickbats and other missiles at them, and the results were that large numbers of the police who had been brought from the Bradford, Leeds, and Keighley districts were fearfully handled. Several of them were struck down the streets and had to be carried to the police-office. Upwards of twenty were injured, some so seriously they had to be conveyed to the Westgate Tavern, where they were attended by the police surgeons. A number of persons were cut about the heads by the police who used their cutlasses. Several were taken to the various surgeries in the town. A number of persons, including several children, had narrow escapes of being trodden to death. From nine o'clock until twelve and throughout the night the town was quiet. The police were stationed in the street until six o'clock yesterday morning. (Bradford Observer, 26 November 1868)

The reported injuries were consistent with being hit by missiles and tussles with rioters – cuts to temples and eyes, bruises to the back, head and arms, twisted ankles and knees and bruised shins.

At the next General Election in 1874, the performance was repeated, with thirty-eight constables wounded, five of whom had also been wounded in 1868.

As well as the right to vote, nineteenth-century workers started to campaign for better pay and conditions, bringing them into conflict with their employers. This increasingly led to a withdrawal of labour when negotiations failed or where wage reductions were proposed. When these industrial disputes became heated, the police were often deployed to try and keep peace and order.

In January 1868, a wage reduction of ten percent was rejected by South Yorkshire's ironworkers, who went on strike for a short period before accepting the reduction to save their jobs. At the same time in the coal industry, prices having stagnated, some colliery owners cut wages by up to twenty-five percent. Brief strikes also took place in some pits in South Wales due to the Welsh miners' aversion to working with Irish colleagues following recent apprehension of Fenian conspirators.

The North Staffordshire miners also staged a brief strike, but it was the striking colliers from Ashton-under-Lyne who caused huge problems for the police, when they joined in a riot provoked by anti-Catholic lectures given by an Irishman named William Murphy.

When a mob of around 1,500 men, armed with sticks and bludgeons, arrived in nearby Dukinfield at 10.30pm on 23 January 1868, they were met by just two police sergeants who attempted to turn them back. The sergeants' efforts being futile, the mob descended on the marketplace and the Roman Catholic chapel, intent on damage. They were persuaded against this, but still seeking trouble the mob set forth for Astley deep pit, where the colliery owner had employed some Staffordshire miners to keep the mine working. By this time, more constables had been rallied to protect the Staffordshire 'nobsticks' and, with physical strength and by threatening to imprison the rioters, kept them at bay for forty-five minutes. The deputy chief constable of Cheshire was sent for and 'with his well-known activity and skill the law was at once set in operation'. Later, eighteen young miners were arrested in their beds for having taken part in the outrage.

On 9 December 1890, Samuel Cunliffe Lister, the owner of Manningham Mills in Bradford, one of the largest mills of its kind in the world, informed workers in his velvet weaving department that, due to the manufactured goods tariff imposed by President McKinley in the USA, he would need to reduce their wages by around twenty percent. It affected around 1,100 of the 5,000 workforce.

Negotiations with management at Manningham failed, and although union officials urged caution, the ill-prepared workers called for strike action. However, a strike fund was established, enabling workers and their families to receive support through food kitchens and extending the strike. By the middle of March 1891, almost the whole workforce was out.

CROWD-CONTROL

Weekly meetings and processions were held in the town centre throughout the strike, occasioning a police presence, although there was little disturbance. However, as the strike strengthened, more constables were assigned to be on duty at the mill:

> *The presence of such vast body of unemployed workpeople in the neighbourhood of the mills must necessarily give for great anxiety, and extra precautions have been deemed necessary. About six o'clock and about nine o'clock this morning there were groups of strikers in the vicinity of the mills, the attitude of some of whom was of a threatening character; but the presence of the police had a deterring effect.* (*Yorkshire Evening Post*, 3 March 1891)

In early April, it was rumoured that up to two thirds of the workforce, who had no actual argument with the management, would return. However, in an about-turn, the spoolers, deciding to show solidarity with their co-workers, refused to return unless the whole spinning department agreed.

Still the management would not budge and the situation came to a climax on 13 April, starting in the afternoon with a mass rally of strikers in front of the town hall.

The disorderly scenes were renewed at 7.30pm, when an enormous crowd gathered and pelted the police with a shower of heavy stones. Mounted constables were summoned, who endeavoured to disperse the angry mob. Shouts of derision greeted the chief constable's warnings of the consequence of a riot, and he and other officers were struck by stones and other missiles, including hammers. One mounted constable's hat was split and his horse fell with him.

Plate-glass windows were smashed and all lamps in the vicinity extinguished, adding to an already difficult situation.

The military had to be summoned, arriving shortly after 9pm and parading the streets and entrances to the main thoroughfares. One or two charges with fixed bayonets were made, although no one was wounded.

Eventually the mayor ascended the steps of the town hall and read the Riot Act, and by 11pm most of the violence had subsided.

However, there were many reports of injuries to both police and public. The chief constable and chief detective inspector both sustained severe facial wounds, and another detective had his horse killed beneath him with a stab wound.

Around twenty rioters were arrested on the spot and taken into custody, others had their names taken for later summonsing. Most of those arrested had been injured, mainly suffering from blows to the head, but one rioter had a main artery and vein cut. This, coupled with treating the wounded police officers who had withdrawn into the town hall, kept two doctors busy all night.

The following morning, an air of considerable excitement and menace prevailed. A large crowd gathered once more, causing further trouble for the police. Troops were still under arms, awaiting an emergency, while those prisoners held in custody were allowed an early breakfast before being brought before the court.

Samuel Cunliffe Lister again found disfavour with his employees during the national miners' strike in 1893. By this time Lister was Lord Masham and as well as being a mill owner, owned the Ackton Hall colliery near Featherstone. The miners' strike was again a reaction against colliery owners' proposed wage reductions, triggered by a drop in coal prices. The lock-out lasted all summer.

In September, the dispute came to a head. As coal was being loaded for transport to Lister's Manningham Mills, a large crowd gathered to try and prevent the coal leaving. The mine manager, sensing trouble, sought assistance from the local police. Unfortunately, 200 constables had already been deployed to the far more pleasurable duty of crowd-control at the three-day Doncaster St Leger race meeting, so thirty soldiers were called in instead. The sight of troops incited the already angry mob of around 2,000 into violent riot, starting fires in the newly built premises and hurling sticks and stones at the vastly out-numbered soldiers. The Riot Act was read and the crowd was instructed to disperse within an hour. After about thirty minutes, a retreat seeming unlikely, soldiers were given the order to charge the crowd with bayonets. The mob returned hurling more stones and in return the military fired several rounds of ball cartridge into the crowd. Eight miners were seriously wounded, two of them, James Gibbs and James Arthur Duggan, fatally.

In the inquiries that followed, the jury found the shooting of Duggan 'justifiable homicide', but Gibbs had been a peaceable man and not involved with any violence. The jury also stated that had the whole district not been deprived of police there would have been no need to call on the military, as the police, assisted by the residents and miners, would have been better able to put down the disturbance without resorting to such extreme measures.

That the police had been more successful at controlling striking miners similarly bent on violent affray was highlighted in other newspaper reports.

In the same week as the riot at Ackton Hall, various newspapers reported:

> *Thousands of miners have surrounded the Neepsend Depot of Manchester, Sheffield, and Lincolnshire Railway to try prevent coal from being taken to its destination, but the carts are effectually guarded by mounted police.* (*Dublin Daily Express*, 8 September 1893)

> *Matters are becoming more and more serious in the Nottingham district. Rioting, orchard robbing, and acts of personal violence perpetrated upon suspected blacklegs, are common occurrences in the extensive coal field to the east of the Leen valley. A number of non-unionists were today forcibly taken from their homes and led through the streets, preceded by a black flag. The leaders of the men however, denounce in strong terms this terrorism, but the men and their wives and children are greatly excited, which has led to numerous violent scenes. At Bulwell, a suburb of Nottingham, where Colonel Seely's men mostly reside, an attack was made upon the weighing machine office. The crowd having smashed the windows, proceeded*

to New Watnall, where they unsuccessfully endeavoured to get the horses out of the pit. In revenge they set fire to the joiner's and blacksmith's shops, further doing great damage to colliery outbuildings before being dispersed by forces of police from Nottingham and Newark. Trucks of coal, lying in sidings, have been overturned and set on fire, and the police stoned when they offered interference. At Watnall pit several men received serious blows, and the situation became so alarming that the County Magistrate was compelled to read the Riot Act. The strikers refusing to disperse, a body of police, reinforced by body from Hull, charged and dispersed the crowd. In the mêlée *Superintendent Harrap, of Newark, was knocked senseless, and twelve constables had be removed to Nottingham Hospital. The wildest excitement prevails.* (*South Wales Daily News*, 8 September 1893)

A renewal of rioting was feared at Morley, and a telegram was sent to York for troops. A further telegram from Leeds states that later the processionists marched along Dewsbury Road and stopped at Chidswell Colliery. News of their approach had been received, and a large force of police was in readiness. On arriving at the colliery the men marched in a body to the gates and demanded an interview with the manager. That gentleman refused to have anything to do with them, and requested the police to keep them back. Capt. Despard divided his men, who were armed with cutlasses, into three detachments, and gave orders to charge. The mob parted in different directions and were eventually scattered. During the conflict several police officers were knocked down and injured, one of them having his head cut open with a stone. The police pursued the crowd along the road for several miles, making repeated charges on those who lagged behind. (*Huddersfield Chronicle*, 8 September 1893)

134

Why the races at Doncaster had required such a large contingent of constables in 1893 is not clear. In previous years, Doncaster Races had been graced with the presence of the Prince of Wales, who attended as the guest of his close friend Mr Christopher Sykes MP of Brantingham Thorpe Hall. Although this was an entirely private arrangement, police attendance had usually been requested to accompany the prince and his entourage, and to clear the way as he travelled from the railway station at Barnby Dun to the racecourse.

This did not always go entirely without incident. In 1878, Constable Lot Moor was on duty when the special train carrying the prince and his distinguished party from Brough Station arrived at Barnby Dun. Awaiting them was a handsome landau with four greys for the prince, and three or four other open carriages, plus a detachment of mounted West Riding Police. Suddenly, one of the carriage horses turned restive and kicked out violently – much to the alarm of the ladies who had just taken their seats. In trying to seize the horse's head, PC Moor was knocked down and severely bruised on the head and ribs, but managed to gain control and help the four occupants to dismount their carriage safely. The remainder of the journey through the crowded traffic passed without incident, and the party arrived at the stand to cheering crowds at 1.30pm.

However, the prince's regular visits to Doncaster ceased, and he was not in attendance in 1893, being at a spa in Homburg, Germany, attempting to lose some of his excess weight.

Public events often drew large crowds, and where these were expected the event organisers requested numbers of police to be deployed to keep the crowd in order.

The duties could include anything from traffic management to ensuring the great and good attending the opening of prestigious buildings were protected from the depredations of bad characters – attracted by the opportunity to pick a few pockets.

In his estimates for the coming year of 1847, the chief constable of Manchester highlighted the time expended by the constables engaged in the numerous special duties of attending public meetings, concerts and theatres and so on. One division alone had seen an average of 6½ constables per day for 7½ hours duty over the previous six months and had also been called upon to provide three constables for the markets for three days a week – the nine-hour trading period meaning those men could not take on any other duty for three days in each week. Although it was his anxious desire not to increase public expenditure on the police unnecessarily, the chief constable felt it his duty to recommend increasing police numbers in order that the people of the town had adequate protection.

As the nation prospered, prestigious public and municipal buildings were constructed apace, especially in the industrial northern towns and cities. Liverpool, Manchester and Bradford opened new concert halls in the early 1850s, concert halls were included in Leeds Town Hall, opened in 1858, and Huddersfield, opened in 1878. Rochdale and Hull completed their new town halls in 1866, while Manchester and Bradford were a little later in the 1870s. In addition to commissioning buildings, councils also purchased areas of land to create public parks to provide green spaces in the otherwise smog-ridden environments.

Peel Park in Bradford, named in honour of Sir Robert, was purchased in 1853 and held its first gala in May, the proceeds of which were to help pay for the new park. The Peel Park Committee requested the attendance of seven constables to help keep the expected crowds in order. Galas became an annual event in Peel Park, usually held at Whitsuntide and always with a police presence, although the numbers of constables required was subsequently left to the discretion of the chief constable to provide 'sufficient number to keep order'.

One event where it might have been expected there would be little trouble – the annual demonstration of the Band of Hope Union in July 1873, an organisation that taught children the importance of sobriety and teetotalism – resulted in Sergeant Samuel Downham being so badly assaulted his ribs were fractured.

Of course, this was not by one of the 30,000 attendees, but by Mr Thackrey, an omnibus conductor in the employment of the Bradford Livery Stable Company, in a traffic incident.

As the gala closed at around 9pm, the constables on duty were trying to control the huge number of cabs, wagonettes and omnibuses awaiting their complement of passengers to take into town. Among these was Mr Thackrey's omnibus, positioned in front of the gates and blocking the whole of one side of the road. The conductor refused the sergeant's repeated requests to move forward, telling him to go to hell. When the sergeant struck the horse on the flanks with a cane, the conductor responded by violently punching the sergeant in the chest, causing him to fall against the pole of a wagonette travelling in the opposite direction.

Thackrey appeared before the magistrates who, after hearing evidence from other cab drivers who contradicted each other, considered the assault proved. Stating as it was the police's duty to keep the road clear, a task that was not easy, the police ought to be protected in the performance of their duty, especially when they were doing it in a proper manner. Deciding a fine was insufficient penalty, the conductor was sentenced to Wakefield House of Correction for two months with hard labour.

Other feasts and fairs requiring policing often saw constables injured in the performance of their duty to control the drunk and disorderly.

Alfred Thornton, a collier, described in the newspaper as a 'rough customer', was committed to a house of correction for seven months for three separate assaults on constables. Thornton, having 'imbibed rather too much liquor', refused to leave Mirfield Feast. When the constables tried to persuade him on his way, he kicked one, bit another and maimed the third. He was eventually overpowered by the aid of some civilians, tied to a cart and taken to a lock-up in Dewsbury.

More pleasant duties included attending the circus when it came to town, and patrolling three-day cricket matches to keep order and protect property.

Extra duties could be profitable too. When Titus Salt requested thirty constables to supervise the fête held in September 1853 to celebrate the opening of the first portion of his vast mill at Saltaire, his generosity – as well as inviting 2,500 of the workforce to a grand luncheon and laying on special trains to take the whole party to a concert in the newly opened St George's Hall in Bradford – extended to a gratuity to each of the constables. No fees or gratuities could be accepted by constables without the permission of the watch committee who in this instance agreed they might be kept, 'they having performed extra duties on the occasion'.

Chapter 10

Police misdemeanours

Not only was alcohol a problem for the ordinary populace, many police constables could not resist its allure either, despite their instruction books plainly forbidding them to enter a public house or accept liquor from anybody when on duty.

In November 1848, after ten months of dealing with cases of drunkenness within the force, Bradford's watch committee decided any officer found in a state of intoxication would be dismissed. The directive was added to the instruction book, and a note was ordered to be pinned in 'a conspicuous place' in the police office.

Even in 1889, the revised Surrey Constabulary's constables' instruction book still found it necessary to reaffirm:

> *If a member of the force be convicted of drunkenness, he will be liable to immediate dismissal, and the plea that the degree of intoxication was slight, will not be considered as any excuse, or avert the punishment which will inevitably follow this offence.*

Punishment seems to have had little effect on sobriety.

It is easy to understand why a constable walking the beat for up to twelve hours through the dark night might wish to partake of a little refreshment before the pubs closed for the night, and again when they re-opened in the early hours of the morning.

The select committee's investigation into intemperance in 1877 highlighted that working men were being tempted into public houses, which opened as early as 6am, and as a result were either going to their employment in a half-stupid state, or not at all. The constable was really no different to his neighbours, except he had few, if any, rest days. And the requirement to be in uniform at all times, on or off duty made him conspicuous.

Many constables were dismissed for parading for duty or coming off duty in an intoxicated state. Those found in beerhouses (and in the company of bad characters and prostitutes) were also dismissed. However, there seem to have been numerous inconsistences in the penalties imposed on drunken constables, many heavily fined or suspended instead of losing their jobs. This may have been a pragmatic approach by watch committees and chief constables, who realised that having trained a constable to some degree of efficiency it might be better to keep him and his habits than to have to replace him with another equally intemperate but untrained man.

Some constables were far more than slightly intoxicated. Disciplinary records describe in colourful detail why their behaviour was brought to the attention of the watch committee.

Just before Christmas in 1886, PC Berriman was found staggering to and fro on the footpath and 'very much the worse for liquor' at 11.45pm. When his sergeant advised he was unfit to work his beat, the constable asserted he had only had two glasses of rum, which he had paid for. Told that he would have to be taken to the central police station, Berriman became aggressive, claiming he was the strongest man in the force and, were he not wearing his uniform, would knock his sergeant out. Somehow, despite Berriman's proclamations of great strength, the sergeant managed to manhandle him to the station. When he later came before the watch committee he was allowed to resign.

Thirteen months later, the same watch committee took a slightly different decision on an intoxicated PC Edgar Balme, who failed to appear when coming off duty at 6am. Hearing reports that a constable had fallen and hurt himself near the gas works, his sergeant and two constables went in search of their injured colleague. On arrival, they found he had been carried into the boiler house of a local foundry. There he lay, dead drunk. A cab was called to transport him to the police station, where the police surgeon, finding the constable helpless and unable to speak, confirmed it was a case of drunkenness. Presumably being speechless meant he could not abuse his superiors and therefore escaped with a week's suspension and a fine of 20 shillings (£111) (around a week's wage).

Even some habitually drunken constables managed to cling on to their jobs, receiving increasingly high fines for each offence. One man lasted twelve years as a constable despite being drunk on duty, under the influence of drink, or neglecting his duty several times. He was also disciplined for immoral conduct, being found in a brewery in the middle of the night, being in a pub in uniform, and for being late on parade on at least a dozen occasions.

One constable, fearful of losing his new job, found the ideal excuse for his apparently intoxicated behaviour. The watch committee, which had heard the charge of his being in liquor, changed its opinion of his misdemeanour when the constable appealed that lightning had affected his sight and caused him to stagger about.

It was not only the lower ranks who succumbed to the temptations of drink.

In October 1842, Superintendent Cyrus Alcock of the Manchester Police was ordered by the new chief constable to attend a special meeting of the watch committee to answer charges that during the previous two-and-a-half years he had frequently been in a state of intoxication. There had been occasions when other officers had needed to assist him to his home, plus stretches of three or four days where he had failed to attend the station and been so incapacitated he could not even sign reports delivered to his home. Not only that, he had forgiven other men for drunkenness and other offences when they should have been reported.

A further three meetings took place to hear and discuss the evidence. Eventually, the watch committee decided that although the superintendent had on certain occasions been seen to be intoxicated, the evidence was insufficient to prove it was a general habit. It was decided that Alcock be demoted to police inspector and his subsequent conduct might enable him to regain the watch committee's full confidence.

That there were inconsistencies in the way constables were disciplined was highlighted in Captain Willis's report, when the chief constable of Manchester undertook his study of the well-established Dublin and London police forces. All three forces had a system whereby the superintendents of their respective divisions could fine or let their men off with a caution, according to how they considered a constable's general behaviour deserved. This power was extended to inspectors in the City of London Police.

It meant there was no uniformity of decisions for offences of similar gravity throughout the forces and opened the door to accusations of favouritism. Some constables asked for transfers to other divisions to remove themselves from the control of stern, overbearing superiors.

Where penalties were decided by a watch committee, compassion was occasionally shown for the home lives of men in the force. If men had lost sleep through caring for sick wives through the night and were late for work, or were drinking to alleviate their anxieties over family members who were ill, a watch committee might consider a reprimand or caution instead of a financial penalty to add to their worries.

However, falling asleep while on the beat always carried a fine.

Some weary constables just fell asleep on walls or in the closet. Others might nod off in the warmth of a designated supper place after a bite to eat. And whether PC Joseph Gowan had been regularly sneaking off for a crafty catnap we cannot know, but having twice been discovered asleep in a cosy corner in the coach house of the police surgeon's residence within two weeks and fined, he probably had to find another spot for his 2am snooze.

Police misdemeanours included 'improper conduct'. Not exactly a crime but classed as misconduct, it usually warranted some disciplinary action – and generally involved unseemly activity with women.

One sergeant, married with a family, was suspended for five nights and fined £2 (£222) for breaching police regulations by irregularly entering a public house. Representing himself as a widower, his mission in going to this pub outside opening hours was to 'pay his addresses' to the widowed landlady.

Two other constables paid a hefty fine for their unofficer-like manner, after Mrs Hill, a beerhouse keeper, complained to the police they had called at her house in the morning and made improper proposals to the female inmates within.

And the stellar career of one officer, who surely should have known better, ended when it emerged he had been engaging in improper conduct with a married woman. Lawrence Nicholas Dyre Hammond was already 42 years old when he joined the police force as a constable. He had served seventeen years in the army, reaching the rank of major, but had no army pension. Quickly rising through the police ranks, he was promoted to superintendent in 1880, but fell from grace in 1898. His compulsory resignation after twenty-three years' service meant he forfeited what would have been a good pension.

As is to be expected of those employed to uphold the law, breaking the law was always a dismissible offence.

Some constables served fewer than six weeks before their nefarious ways were uncovered and they were dismissed. Charles Sedgewick only served thirty days before it came to the attention of the force that he had previously kept a public house, which was the resort of thieves. As he too had been suspected of committing a felony, he was dismissed and never afforded the opportunity to use his insider knowledge in conducting his police duties.

PC Edwin Parson took advantage of his powers of search to steal a snuff box and 7 shillings (£39) from a drunken man, asleep at the roadside. After a criminal trial at the sessions, he was sentenced to nine months in gaol.

Some stole food from the people they lodged with, others appropriated clothing and accoutrements from the police force. Others used their privileged position of trust to rob the businesses they were supposed to be protecting – and were sentenced to several years' penal servitude.

Accusations of the police's ill-treatment of members of the public, either verbally or physically, were frequent. It seems complainants who were better educated or held public office were more likely than the working classes to have their grievances heard.

After the nationwide municipal elections of 1891, Bradford's watch committee received a deputation from the now ex-councillor Mr Joseph Smith, a Liberal, and other ratepayers, complaining that numerous constables, in attendance at the town hall during the elections, had jeered and hurled abuse at Smith and two newly elected Conservative councillors. What had provoked this unseemly outburst is unclear, although the electorate had just returned a landslide victory for the Conservative party in the borough, which may not have pleased the police. The constables, also attending the committee meeting, expressed regret and stated they had already sent written apologies to the councillors. However, proper though the apologies were, the committee resolved that a gross breach of police duty had been committed. It expressed its great displeasure at the constables' misbehaviour, which was totally without excuse. Superintendent Byng, also on duty at the time, was severely reprimanded for lacking discipline and his failure to immediately suppress the disorderly conduct.

And when Emanuel Birkbeck wrote to the *Manchester Courier* of his experience of unnecessary police violence against him in April 1869, he probably spoke for the hundreds of those less articulate persons who had received similar treatment.

His only 'crime' was to have challenged Sergeant Carr, who was supervising the extinguishing of a large warehouse fire in Manchester's Caernarvon Street. A large crowd of excited observers had gathered to watch proceedings and this was clearly irritating to the sergeant, who was 'being very noisy and rough with the bystanders and using unnecessary language'. Venturing to ask the sergeant to be a little more civil and not so sharp, Mr Birkbeck was threatened with being locked up if he said anything else. Undeterred, Mr Birkbeck retorted: 'You will not and if you are not more civil I will take your number.' At which point the sergeant ordered him to be arrested by a 'tall young man in civilian clothes'.

Mr Birkbeck was unceremoniously dragged from the crowd,

'pulled about and ill-used, and taken through the streets like a felon of the deepest dye' to the police station. Fortunately for Mr Birkbeck, his plight had been witnessed by a gentleman who rushed out in his slippers to accompany the men to the police station. Mr Birkbeck was detained in a cell containing 'a wife-beater [another man] and a closet', until a charge could be drummed up against him. His witness was expelled from the station.

Charged with assaulting a policeman, he eventually managed to get word to his wife and friends, who stood his bail. At the magistrates' court next morning, it was alleged by Sergeant Carr and the constable who had taken him into custody that Mr Birkbeck had been shoving and pushing the men in charge of the fire hose, and had struck both sergeant and constable in the chest.

But once again his last-minute witness came to Mr Birkbeck's rescue, telling the court no such thing had happened, that the sergeant had been abusive to the crowd, and it was Mr Birkbeck who had been roughly used.

The case was dismissed, but Mr Birkbeck was justifiably angry and indignant. He wrote:

> *After this how is a man safe in the street, however respectable? Had it not been for a stranger running after me, fortunately leaving his name and address at the station, and appearing in court as a witness of the circumstances, and for the most exemplary conduct of my employers, the probability is that I might either have been mulcted* [penalised by] *in a heavy fine or sent to prison, with loss of situation, character, good opinion, and everything that is dear to a respectable citizen. As a ratepayer I thought I was entitled to rebuke his palpably gross demeanour towards the people; if not, we are bound to submit to anything they choose to do towards us, however willing and desirous we are to assist them in their duties. I have had the matter before Captain Palin, but under legal advice withdrew from another engagement. I*

145

find in action at law I could obtain substantial redress for false imprisonment from Sergeant Carr, providing he had the means: but, after investigation, my adviser cannot find that he could pay costs; so that after all, a person may be taken through the streets, kept in prison for hours, not allowed to seek witnesses, and should any persons tender themselves as such they must expect to receive nothing but insult and ruffianly treatment, and not one sufferer can obtain redress. Armed and protected by the authorities, looked upon in every possible way agents of the law, the least police officers can do is to speak the truth but as they will not, it would be wise to consider how this institution can be practicably reformed. I have been deeply injured, still feel a sufferer, and as a citizen it is my duty to offer the widest possible publicity. (Manchester Courier, 21 April 1869)

Although Mr Birkbeck may not have been able to access any compensation or proper justice for his rough treatment at the hands of the police, at least he could make his voice heard, unlike some boys taking a swim in a canal who were pelted with stones by the police.
A sergeant and two constables were brought before Manchester's City Police Court charged with assaulting a lad who was bathing with his friends. Although a doctor who examined the boy had needed to attend to his injuries for five or six days – because he was exhausted, frightened and sometimes delirious – attested there were deep marks on the boy's back, bruises and cuts on his hip, and a black mark on his arm, it was insinuated the wounds were caused through a fall and not by the violently thrown stones.

It was agreed throwing stones – a violation of the law – was an improper thing for a police officer to do, but was an indiscretion rather than great misconduct. In summing up, the chairman of the bench said:

He was very glad that this case, which for time had caused great sensation, and had been called a brutal assault by

146

*the police, should have turned out to be a very trifling
matter indeed. It seemed that these children caused great
annoyance by bathing in the canal, and that the police had
very great difficulty preventing them from bathing there.*
(*Manchester Courier*, 28 July 1866)

One constable was fined 10 shillings (£55.50) for his indiscretion, the
case against the other two men being dismissed – and it was hoped the
authorities would take no further notice of the matter.

One brutal assault by police reported in the *Yorkshire Post* of 27 July
1895 was not heard in court, but at a protracted sitting of the watch
committee, where the police surgeon was called to give evidence on
the extent of the injuries inflicted on the victims.

This serious incident, in which the police wrongfully arrested and
beat four men, did result in the dismissal of a sergeant and eight
constables. The men, members of the Bradford Borough Police Force
cricket team, were returning by wagonette from a match at Guiseley
at around 11.30pm. Presumably, by the late hour and their subsequent
lack of judgement, they had partaken of a celebratory post-match
drink. As they travelled along Canal Road, they were hailed by two
young lads aged 15 and 16, who had been working at a local mill
until 11.15pm and were sheltering from the rain under a railway arch.
Because of the inclement weather they had covered their heads with
sacking – the police bizarrely using this in defence, 'believing them
to be dressed as women'. The wagonette driver ignored them but
cheekily the lads climbed onto the back, intending to hitch a lift into
the town centre. At this point the police began to beat them with
sticks (perhaps believing them to have malicious intent), knocking
the lads into the road. The wagonette stopped, the police alighted
and carried on rough-handling the lads. Hearing screams, a
greengrocer and his son rushed to the lads' assistance, but also took
a beating from the police. The police arrested all four men, taking
them into custody at the main police station in the town hall,
charging them with loitering with intent to commit felony. His

suspicions aroused about the nature of the occurrence, the superintendent released the prisoners and reported the matter to his chief constable.

After evidence was presented to support the charges of falsely apprehending and grossly assaulting the men, the watch committee decided unanimously to dismiss all nine policemen – the sacking carrying with it the loss of all money paid into the superannuation fund, a considerable sum in some cases.

Chapter 11

Improving the policeman's lot

One of the key provisos in the establishment of police forces nationally in 1856 was the requirement for each police force to be efficient. To ensure competency, every force was to be inspected annually by the newly created Inspectorate of Constabulary.

Forces had a financial incentive to comply, as being certified as efficient meant the Treasury would meet a quarter of the costs of the pay and clothing of the men.

Section 15 of the County and Borough Police Act stipulated three people to be appointed as inspectors to:

> *Visit and inquire into the State and the Efficiency of the Police appointed for every County and Borough, and whether the Provisions of the Acts under which such Police are appointed are duly observed and carried into effect, and also into the State of the Police Stations, Charge Rooms, Cells, or Lock-ups, or other Premises occupied for the Use of such Police.*

The first three inspectors were John Woodford, chief constable of Lancashire Constabulary, Major General William Cartwright of Flore House, Northamptonshire – a man with wide experience of judicial and financial matters – and Captain Edward Willis, Manchester's chief constable.

In early 1857, Cartwright made a preliminary inspection of the twenty-five counties under his remit, finding that of the fifteen forces established prior to the 1856 Act, only nine could be considered efficient.

Official inspections commenced in earnest in late 1857. All three men were thorough, visiting almost every station and lock-up of every force, however small.

There was no clear definition of efficiency, though the Act did set out certain conditions for issuing a certificate of efficiency for those forces found to be efficient in 'point of numbers and discipline'.

The inspectors focused on four parameters:

- The strength of the force in terms of numbers.
- The ratio of police officers to population.
- The quality of supervision exercised over the officers.
- The degree of co-operation given to neighbouring forces.

Although the 1839 County Police Act had stipulated a ratio of police to population of at least one police officer to every 1,000 inhabitants, the required ratio in towns and boroughs was questioned by Woodford. The response from Grey, the home secretary, was vague:

> *The Home Secretary could not give any sanction to the rule that a police force is to be considered sufficient in point of numbers if it is in the proportion of one man to a thousand, and he thinks although it is possible that in some places that might be a sufficient number, experience has shown that in towns with a large and dense population a larger proportion is requisite.*[34]

Quality of supervision and efficient discipline was also tricky to assess. The inspectors used the ratio of superior officers to constables on duty as a measure to ascertain whether or not there were sufficient officers to continuously and regularly supervise the men under their charge. Pressure was brought to bear on forces where the ratio of police to population (using the 1851 census as a guide) was deemed too low. By threatening the loss of the Treasury grant, the inspectors successfully persuaded several authorities to increase police numbers. Where it was found to be lacking, supervision was addressed, with extra tiers of 'management' being recruited in some forces, and additional superintendents in others.

That the country did not have a standardised police system was evident from the first reports. Variations across forces were pronounced. Pay scales were widely different: leadership and outlook affected their efficiency too.

The inspectors, therefore, had to apply a degree of flexibility in their assessments, considering the needs of each locality and whether its police force was adequate to combat crime in that area. Complete eradication of crime was not expected.

County forces were less problematic than the 208 borough forces. Some of the larger cities had good police to population ratios – even in 1856, Manchester had one police officer for every 540 people, and Liverpool's ratio was 1:393. But in Huddersfield, the chief constable reported a strength of sixty-eight men to police the borough's 70,000 inhabitants in 1870, and as late as 1882 the prosperous and rapidly expanding borough of Bradford, with a population of almost 200,000, had a strength of force of only 220.

Bradford did seek to make amends to this deficit, noting there had been no increase in police numbers in the previous six years – despite a growth in population of thirty-four percent, 14 miles of new streets being laid out and the construction of more than 3,500 additional houses, warehouses and other buildings, all of which needed to be watched and protected. The watch committee proposed to recruit a further twenty men.

Bradford and Huddersfield were just two of the majority of the fifty-seven large boroughs, so defined by their populations in excess of 20,000, regarded as efficient, despite the less than ideal strength of force. However, some forces still had not achieved efficiency by 1870, and these included Macclesfield established in 1836, and Ashton under-Lyne and its neighbours Oldham and Stockport.

A more tangible aspect of inspection was the number and standard of police buildings. Many lacked adequate facilities for both police personnel and those in custody, and improvement programmes had to be implemented in many forces over a period of several years. The new police station for Manningham, Bradford, was described in glowing terms in the *Leeds Times* of 28 April 1877:

> *The new building is a handsome structure externally and internally it is commodious. It is built of stone with a high pitched roof and the north-east corner has a round tower with a spirelet surmounted with a highly ornamental iron finial and vane. Separate entrances are provided for the police department and to the house of the sub-inspector, as the officers are now styled. The police office and parade room for the men is a well-lighted, lofty room, and adjacent are 4 cells, warmed with hot water and ventilated; and on the west side is an engine house in which is placed the diminutive fire engine, supposed to be used in case of any fire in Manningham, but really of no practical value in the event of a fire of any magnitude. The Watch Committee are also having built in Leeds Road a police station for that district; and although this structure is less pretentious than that at Manningham it is roomy and comfortable.*

During the inspections, Major Cartwright identified other points needing rectification, and these became key goals for the inspectorate's aim of achieving an efficient police service throughout the country.

As well as provision of decent police stations, accommodation, cells and lock-ups, these included uniformity of pay scales nationally and a settled pension scheme, given as a right instead of being discretionary.

Establishing the pension scheme was a priority. County constabularies had been obliged to create superannuation funds under Section 11 of the amended County Police Act in 1840, but there was no such compulsion for the borough forces where town councils, being merely *enabled* to set up funds for employees, rarely did so.

With most boroughs having no pension fund, Cartwright believed it necessary for a new Act of Parliament to address the problem. Thus, the County and Borough Police Act of 1859 included making it compulsory for borough forces to establish police superannuation funds.

Although mandatory, many borough councils showed reluctance to establish a superannuation fund, procrastinating for months, repeatedly referring the matter back to the watch committee. This disinclination might have been due to the declaration in the eighth section of the Act that each council would have to guarantee the security of the fund and make good any shortfall from the borough fund or rates. Where new funds were being established, the likelihood of there being a greater call on the fund than the monies so far accrued was significant. Besides, the contributory nature of the fund was likely to result in a request by police officers for salary increases – something councils sought to avoid.

On 21 January 1860, Bradford's town clerk was instructed to send circulars of enquiry to other boroughs regarding the new Act, specifically the establishment of a superannuation fund. A month later a sub-committee was set up to 'consider and report on scales of deductions from wages and allowances to Police Constables from the superannuation fund to be formed under the Police Act 1859'.[35]

Nothing much seems to have been done. Eighteen months later, at the watch committee's meeting of 1 July 1861, the town clerk narrated a letter from the Home Office requesting the council's attention be called to the formation of a superannuation fund and the imperative requirements of the Act of Parliament.

A fortnight later the watch committee recommended a superannuation fund be formed at rates it had already recommended on 15 November 1859.

After another month, another new sub-committee formed to once again consider the subject and a week later reported:

> *Having sought the opinions of all the town councils in England and Wales having a police force of 15 men and upwards upon the compulsory provisions of the Police Counties and Boroughs Act 1859 with reference to*

> *formation of a superannuation fund and having considered*
> *the replies received it is the opinion of this committee that*
> *it not be expedient at present for the council to take any*
> *measure for the repeal of the Act or of the compulsory*
> *provisions thereof, since it does not appear, from the*
> *answers that have been received to the enquiries of this*
> *council that any such measure would receive the general*
> *support of other town councils.*[36]

A deduction of 2.5% of each man's salary was agreed – the highest amount allowable in the legislation – and the fund was up and running by the next presentation of accounts in October 1861.

It also started to pay out. Sergeants Joseph Jennings, John Knowles and John Walsh being 'worn out and disabled from infirmity of body' were superannuated at 14 shillings a week each (£77.70), being half of their pay. Constables Jacob Hayter and John Whitaker similarly received allowances of 12 shillings a week (£66.60).

Bradford was not alone in its delay. The inspections of 1860–61 revealed there were thirty-one other non-compliant boroughs.

In contrast, Manchester (under the enlightened chief constable-ship of Edward Willis) had the foresight in 1845 for:

> *A "Superannuation or Police Relief Fund" [to] be at once*
> *established for the purpose of providing a fund, out of*
> *which may be paid to members of the Police Force who*
> *may receive injuries in the service, or on retirement after*
> *long and faithful service, such remuneration either in the*
> *form of gratuity, or an annual allowance, as the committee*
> *may consider they are entitled to receive.*[37]

It took just two months to agree a one percent contribution from all ranks and the fund be supplemented by:

> *[...] all moneys received for the service of Summonses and*
> *Warrants by the Police, from the sale of old Police*

clothing, unclaimed and stolen property recovered by the
Police and forfeited, also the amount accruing from fines
imposed for assaults on Police Constables, together with
such other sums as it may be lawful for the Council or the
Committee to pay or direct to be paid in aid of the said
relief fund, shall be so applied and paid into an account
to be entitled "The Manchester Police Relief Fund
Account."[38]

Guidelines to assist the watch committee in granting annuities and
allowances from Manchester's fund were laid down as follows:

Every member of the Force who shall have served with
diligence and fidelity upwards of 20 years, and who shall
from infirmity of mind or body have become unable to
discharge the duties of his Office, shall be eligible to be
placed on the Superannuation List with an annual
allowance from the said Fund of such some not being more
than two thirds of his pay, as the Watch Committee may
determine.

A gratuity may be granted out of the said fund to any
member of the Force who may be worn out after diligent and
faithful service of less than 15 years, but upwards of 8 years
in the proportion of one month's full pay for every year's
service, or such other sum, not exceeding that amount, as
the Watch Committee may think expedient to grant.

Every member of the Force who shall be disabled by
bodily injuries received in the execution of his duty shall
be eligible to be placed on the Superannuated List with an
annual allowance from the said Fund of such sum not
exceeding three fourths of his pay, as the Watch Committee
may consider the circumstances of the case require.

In the event of any member of the Force being killed or
dying from the effects of wounds received in the execution
of his duty, his widow if any (or family in case his wife be

dead leaving a family, then the children) so long as the widow remains unmarried, and continues respectable in her conduct, so long as the Committee may determine, such annual sum not exceeding three fourths of the pay of the deceased as the Committee may determine.

The length of service shall be calculated from the time any member of the Force first entered into the Police either under the authorities of the Borough, or any of the Townships within the Borough, provided he has, without any interruption, continued a member of the Police Force, either of the Townships or the Borough.

Since police forces continued to be under local control and funding, it is little wonder superannuation funds varied widely across the country by the 1870s.

Somerset Constabulary reported a healthy fund of over £14,925 (£1,656,675), with yearly receipts of almost £1,849 (£205,240) and charges on the fund of only £160 (£17,760) per year. The City of Bath's force also had a relatively healthy fund of £8,100 (£900,000) with annual income of around £407 (£45,000). But with annual payments of pensions and gratuities exceeding £438 (£48,600), the statement warned the fund would eventually be depleted and would need to be supplemented from the rates. In real poverty was Bedfordshire's fund standing at just under £11 (£1,220), and with a tiny income to fund its one pensioner.

There was real concern that many funds were either insolvent or on the verge of being so. Men also objected to being compelled to contribute to funds they might not ultimately derive any benefit from if they were dismissed or resigned. Some believed they could be dismissed at the whim of a chief constable just before they were eligible to draw their pension.

In March 1875, a select committee was established 'to inquire into the Police Superannuation Funds in the Counties and Boroughs of England and Wales'. It was two years before it published its report of twenty foolscap pages.

IMPROVING THE POLICEMAN'S LOT

The *Liverpool Mercury* of 28 April 1877 shrewdly summed up the state of affairs, criticising the patchwork ways in which institutions were brought into existence with:

> *[L]egislature too timid to do more than yield a little at a time to the demands made upon its regenerative powers, the consequence being that session after session is wasted in pottering with inefficient measures passed in previous sessions; in botching and repairing, consolidating and extending, instead of building anew and turning out original work.*

The editorial described the select committee as being 'charged with the duty of organising an intelligible and workable system of superannuation for the various police forces throughout England and Wales', highlighting the problems of the different systems between county and borough forces, both for collecting funds and granting pensions and gratuities. The existing system of police superannuation, it said, 'was a muddle':

> *Perhaps it was too much to expect that the originators of our modern police system should have turned out a piece of machinery absolutely complete in every particular; but after having first made the establishment of local police forces permissive and then compulsory, first in the boroughs and afterwards in the counties, and after having made three or four separate attempts to found an efficient superannuation scheme, one would have scarcely thought Parliament would have been troubled between thirty and forty years afterwards to take in hand and complete the job so ineffectually dealt with by its predecessors.*

In a press release sent by special telegram, the select committee had stated:

157

In their opinion the simplest as well as the soundest course would be to make the pensions a direct charge upon the rates, protecting the men by a fixed scale and by appeal, and for the future that those contributions, whether from the men or from other sources, which at present go in support of the superannuation funds, should be paid into the police and borough rates of the several localities, whilst to avoid as far as possible the present ratepayer benefitting unfairly as against the ratepayer of the future, all accumulated funds should be converted into the terminable annuities, for the benefit of the rates of the localities where they exist. With a view of carrying this proposal into effect, it is recommended the existing enactments, relating to the contributions to the funds or to the pensions of the men, should be repealed, and a measure be introduced making the pensions of the police a direct charge upon the rates, establishing a scale and regulations to which those persons may be obtained, together with other minor changes recommended by the committee.

It recommended adopting the principle that a claim to a fixed pension after a given number of years' service should be recognised as a right, and suggested this should be fifteen-fiftieths after fifteen years (with a medical certificate to prove permanent incapacity), rising by one-fiftieth each year to twenty years and two-fiftieths to twenty-five years (unconditional), and one-fiftieth to twenty-eight years, when a pension of two-thirds salary was attained. This mirrored the system in the Metropolitan Police Force.

However, although Bills were introduced into the House of Commons in 1882, 1883, 1884 and 1885, little progress was made in pushing the recommendations through Parliament.

Finally, thirteen years after the report, a Bill was passed on Tuesday 5 August 1890, becoming known as the Police Act 1890, giving a decent pension as a right to a policeman retiring after twenty-five years of service.

This did not go down well in quarters outside the police service. The *Hull Daily Mail* received several letters of which it printed just one:

> *Sir, I think it has hardly been realised what enormous advantages the present Government Bill will give the police, over every other branch of the Civil Service, in the way of pensions. For a first-class constable the bill would provide, at two-fifths pay, about £40 to £45 per year for life after 25 years' service; sergeants would receive about £55 and inspectors from £70 to £90 a year for life. If they enter the service at 21 they might retire at 46, so practically in the prime of life, with a chance of earning a good income in addition. Is it true 2 or 2.5% is deducted from their pay? I wonder if they have ever cast out what this would come to? In the case of a constable who had 9d week deducted, it would leave him, if capitalised and invested, at the end of 25 years with an income as a pension of about £4 per annum, instead of from £40 to £45. So that the more one looks into it the more munificent is the scale. – I am sir, your obedient servant, PENSIONER.*

When the Act came into force on 1 April 1891, it allowed constables and sergeants over the age of 55 and higher ranks over 60 to retire without a medical certificate.

It meant PC Thomas Bottomley aged 69 (and now referred to as 'Old Bott' by the criminal fraternity) could finally retire after thirty-nine uninterrupted years of pounding his Manningham beat. He must have immediately given his required one month's notice as on 30 April 1891, two weeks after the Manningham Mills strike ended, he was superannuated at 20s 8d a week (£115), exactly two-thirds of his merit constable's salary of 31 shillings (£175). The *Yorkshire Evening Post* of 14 May 1891, reported:

PRESENTATION TO A BRADFORD POLICE OFFICER
On Wednesday night there was an interesting gathering of
police officials at the Manningham Police Station,
Bradford, the occasion being the retirement after thirty-
nine years' service in the force, of Constable Bottomley. As
a mark of the respect entertained for him by his brother
officers, a handsome ivory-mounted ebony walking stick
was presented to Mr Bottomley. Inspector Jackman made
the presentation, and Sub-Inspector Bentley also offered
some appropriate observations.

He was fortunate in enjoying a retirement of fourteen years, probably receiving around twenty-times his financial contribution.

Holidays and rest days, paid or unpaid, seem to have been at the discretion of individual forces. In the early days, most policemen worked a seven-day week, although Birkenhead introduced the idea of police being 'released from duty' in 1841. They were allowed four rest days per year, without pay, and only providing they left their uniforms with their superintendent. Things improved slightly for the Birkenhead men in 1855 when the force introduced three days paid annual leave to 'those members of the Force who shall have conducted themselves to the satisfaction of the Committee for twelve months'.[39]

In late 1878, Bradford issued new regulations stipulating all policemen be allowed one day off in fourteen and all ranks below superintendent would have seven days paid leave per year. This was increased in 1893 to ten days for sergeants and inspectors, bringing them in line with the holiday entitlement for superintendents.

Paid holidays for the Cheshire Constabulary seem to have been more generous than Bradford's as, in 1891, its superintendent had twenty-one days paid leave, inspectors fourteen and other ranks ten. However, they only had one day off per month and worked a nine-hour day.

All was not quite as well in Middlesbrough, though. Even as late as 1893, William Ashe, the mean-spirited Middlesbrough chief constable, referring to the agitation amongst the constabulary for a day's holiday per month, reported to the watch committee:

With respect to the application of the constables for an additional leave of absence of one day per month, I cannot recommend it be granted, unless the committee can see their way to augment the force by three more constables, because as at present there are not more than are necessary for the efficient working of the borough. During the summer months an average five men are off duty every week, on their annual leave, besides other men off duty on the sick list, and from the return I lay before you, you will notice that sickness is a heavy item. I may also state that in the memorial presented by the constables, no mention is made of the allowance of half an hour every night to each man for supper, which deducted from the eight hours for the 26 weeks' night duty, makes eleven days. This is a privilege which scarcely any other force enjoys. (*Daily Gazette for Middlesbrough*, 6 May 1893)

The committee adopted the chief constable's recommendation and one might suppose sickness levels increased further as a consequence.

Hours of work varied too, and though progress was slow in some forces, improvements were gradually made. Bradford's force still worked on a 2 x 12-hour shift system when the watch committee was petitioned in 1889 asking the daily duty to be fixed at eight hours. In its usual style the committee sought information from other principal boroughs and gave the matter careful consideration. Deciding that since arrangements in other boroughs depended on their individual circumstances and Bradford's system was already the best it could be to protect life and property in the town efficiently, the request was refused. In 1891, the watch committee reviewed the matter and eventually agreed to an eight-hour working day – although this was not implemented for a further year.

Since police officers were frequently in need of medical attention, either through general sickness or through injuries sustained while on duty, access to treatment was a key welfare concern.

Again, forward-thinking Birkenhead, although a relatively small force of only thirty men, appointed Dr Jennette as police surgeon in 1844 at a salary of £10 per year (£1,110). This cost was covered by a deduction of 2d a week from each man's wage (92p).

Dr Jennette remained in post for forty years, and was succeeded by Dr Cornwall in 1885. At this time the chief constable pointed out that weekly deductions were higher than those paid into local sick clubs and recommended they be reduced to 1d a week (46p).

One condition laid down by Bradford's borough force in 1848 was that each constable must produce a certificate to prove he had become a member of a mutual benefit society or sick club within two months of his appointment to the force. Failure to do so would result in his dismissal. However, when it appointed Dr Parkinson as police surgeon in 1867, the watch committee provided access to free general healthcare and emergency medical attention to all force members. Although there were costs of around £80 per year (£8,880) involved in tending to sick and injured men, the benefits of them being able to return more quickly to their duties probably outweighed the expense.

Recognising training and personal development would help constables to not only gain promotion but also make them better preservers of the peace and ultimately increase job satisfaction, some forces introduced training classes, as well as providing reading rooms and material to encourage men to learn.

Incredibly for a city and force the size of Manchester, no special classes existed for the benefit of members who wished to improve themselves educationally until 1899.

The new chief constable, Robert Peacock, who had worked his way up through the police ranks with previous experience as chief constable of Canterbury and then Oldham, took over the running of the force after his predecessor, Charles Malcolm Wood, had allowed a corrupt system to flourish. Wood's authoritarian policing methods had taken no account of the tribulations of the men on the beat and there had been little learning and not much improvement in the men's supervision. Peacock sought to turn around his failing force by introducing promotional exams and educating the men.

On 15 September 1899, he addressed the force in the lord mayor's parlour in Manchester Town Hall as he instigated a series of training lectures and educational classes for the first time. That these were for the police only was with good reason:

> *It would certainly not be advisable in the interests of the force for constables to attend classes where they would be compelled to associate with persons with whom they would frequently come into contact when on duty in the street, as the less close association between civilians and constables the better it is for the force both collectively and individually. I do not say you should not have friendships and associations with civilians, but an association such as would follow from mixed attendance at public evening classes would not be conducive to the efficient discharge of your duty in the streets as occasions would undoubtedly arise when your duty might be in conflict with the conduct of your associates of the class or of their friends, and in either case their presence and influence would not render the discharge of your duty any easier. Again a large percentage of the students in attendance at public evening classes are boys and youths and it would be most unpleasant for constables to have to mingle with the youths and later be subject to the annoyance of being pointed out in the streets. We know the boys are a sufficient annoyance at present without giving them additional material to annoy policemen with and it is pretty certain that if you attended mixed classes where boys are present they would undoubtedly make you a mark for cheap wit whenever they saw you in the street, and this*

163

I know very well would not only be most annoying but also very discouraging to you and probably lead to you giving up attendance in disgust.[40]

Recognising that current policemen whose boyhoods twenty or thirty years earlier had been at a time when free education was not widely available, the objective of the classes was to bring the men to the same intellectual standards as the rising educated generation from which the criminal fraternity was now emerging:

You must remember many of the criminals of today possess more or less of education but unfortunately for the police use their knowledge and abilities for most improper purposes. As you are aware they consequently show far more ingenuity and skill in the pursuit of a criminal career than did their predecessors in past years and this means if you are to successfully cope with them and efficiently protect the public you must be of equal, if not superior, education to them. If you are not you will be placed at enormous disadvantage when dealing with this class of criminal and you will stand a very poor chance of successfully meeting them. This is even more important with regard to detection of crime and prevention of it.[41]

Writing clear reports and presenting concise evidence was also key to increasing the value of the policeman's work, and the art would be acquired by careful study:

Personally I am looking forward to a time in the near future when every man will be able to write and compose properly completed reports. Every police officer before he can be considered efficient should be able to do that but I'm sorry to have to admit that at present there are members of this force who cannot produce an ordinary report in anything like an intelligent or satisfactory manner.

An ignorant policeman is no credit to himself or to his uniform or the town which he serves. Education not only enables a constable to perform his duties satisfactorily to the public and more creditably to himself but also benefits him personally by increasing his chances of promotion, by enlarging his views and knowledge generally, by raising him orally, intellectually and socially, and by rendering him an intelligent and thinking being.[42]

Impressing upon the men that the classes were established for their own benefit and not Peacock's, the men were expected to attend classes three nights a week and diligently pursue their studies at home on the remaining evenings to derive full benefit from the exceptional privilege afforded to them.

Two hundred and sixty men initially signed up for the classes, which were expected to continue for five years.

It is indicative of the issues still facing the police that the first few lectures focused on the licensing laws and carried the admonition:

[...] 9/10ths of the men who have been dismissed or called upon to resign have had to leave directly as a consequence of taking too much drink. Let this be a warning to you as, without doubt, indulgence in intoxicating liquor when on duty will in the long run bring ruin both to yourselves and your families.[43]

Life was not just slog, sweat and study for police force members, though. Working alongside colleagues on a daily basis for many hours, then, as now, resulted in the development of close friendships (and otherwise) and a general camaraderie, heightened by the challenging circumstances of their common purpose.

Police teamwork was vital in fighting and solving crime, particularly when faced with dangerous situations, and participation in sports and social clubs, such as cricket and football teams and in choirs and bands, strengthened those bonds. Events and outings also provided the opportunity for wives and families to be involved and make friends.

A particularly gratifying day out was had by the men, families and friends of the Bromley Police Force, during a day out to Hampton Court coupled with a cricket match in August 1893. The party travelled through glorious Kent and Sussex countryside in three specially chartered brakes on a beautiful summer's morning, accompanied by lively music from the musicians on board.

The correspondent noted that 'Master Robert', once he had cast aside his cumbersome quasi-military helmet and regulation dress – which was awe-inspiring to all naughty boys and evil-doers – like other human beings had a heart beating beneath his coat of blue and: 'his experience of the shadows of life had not yet succeeded in making quite the misanthrope of him. Oh yes, a policeman knew how to enjoy life just as well as anybody else.' (*Bromley & District Times*, 18 August 1893)

The excursion stopped at a coaching inn for glasses of beer and cheese and biscuits before speeding onward through busy Croydon, Morden and Morton, eventually alighting at Hampton Court. An innings of cricket between the police and tradesmen was played, before a break for lunch and post-prandial speeches at the Kings Arms. While the cricketers continued their match in broiling heat, those with better things to do either visited the palace, strolled in the park or took boat trips on the Thames. Leaving Hampton at 7pm, the party arrived back in Bromley marketplace just before midnight and joined in a verse of *Auld Lang Syne*.

A similar occasion saw the Southampton Borough Police visit Lyndhurst in the New Forest for a cricket match against the New Forest division of the Hampshire Constabulary in August 1876. While the match was proceeding, those not playing attended to the wants of the wives, children and sweethearts. Everyone adjourned for a 'capital tea' at the Crown Hotel, before ladies and children were dispatched to Southampton at 7pm.

As soon as the ladies had departed, the men and players repaired to the new dining room for a first-rate dinner, where no doubt ribald banter took place between the opposing teams. During the toasts the vice-chairman of the New Forest team told of the pleasure there was in meeting their friends from Southampton in the cricket field, since they had often to meet them in connection with their duty. He believed:

> *Cricket matches did much to bring about a right state of feeling among them, which must tend for the benefit of the public. There were 40,000 policemen in the country, and comparison with other bodies brought them out very favourably indeed, while the support the police now received from the public, contrasted with what they formerly had, showed their services were appreciated by those who watched them very narrowly.* (*Hampshire Advertiser*, 19 August 1876)

The evening was spent in a convivial and enjoyable manner, ending at 11pm. with the National Anthem. Cheers were given for the Southampton men as they took their departure for their borough, where they arrived soon after midnight, having enjoyed a most delightful day in a pretty part of the New Forest.

Regular cricket matches between the police forces of Hull and Bradford engendered mutual co-operation, not only between members of the force but also between the dignitaries of the two boroughs.

In June 1878, Hull invited the Bradford team and various townsmen of both towns to participate in a match against its newly established cricket team at the Hull Town ground. The match, attended by 1,000 people, was preceded by breakfast for players and dignitaries at the Royal Station Hotel. After the match – won by Hull who had borrowed two of Bradford's players – a dinner was hosted by the Mayor of Hull, who hoped there would be a return fixture the following year.

In fact, the next meeting came much earlier, when the Bradford men, wishing to reciprocate the kind hospitality they had received, invited the Hull team and entourage to visit Bradford for a return match that August. Understanding the importance of fostering the relationship, liberal subscriptions flowed in from the mayor and magistrates, solicitors and others. The Hull party arrived in Bradford by train at 10am. While the cricketers were taken to the ground at Undercliffe, the Hull gentlemen walked to the town hall to meet the mayor and other corporation dignitaries. They were given a tour of the town and served lunch before joining the numerous spectators assembled at Undercliffe. Again the Hull team was victorious.

At 5.30pm, the players and guests adjourned to the Peel Park Hotel for 'an excellent dinner' and to commit to a further contest the following summer when Bradford's cricketers would endeavour to give the Hull team 'a right good thrashing!'

As well as fostering good relationships between different forces, sporting events could be fundraisers to benefit good causes. The police in Huddersfield hosted a charity match against the Nottinghamshire Constabulary to raise funds for Huddersfield Infirmary in July 1876. The match was well-attended by the public as well as by senior members of other police forces. During the post-match dinner, the chairman stated his belief that such matches created a good feeling between the various police forces in the country. He opined that as a body of men, he did not know of any who needed enjoyment more than policemen, adding if people who held the opinion that policemen did no work had to walk about the streets day after day, night after night, and week after week, as the policemen had to do, they too would need recreation.

Huddersfield borough police force excelled themselves in fundraising again in January and April 1896, when their rugby team twice took on a team of 'Old Fossils' to raise money for the first horse ambulance in the borough. The sum required was around £170 (£19,000), the ambulance being rather grander than most.

Built by a local firm of eminent carriage-makers, Messrs Rippon, the new ambulance was described as being built of well-seasoned Newfoundland birch and dark American walnut, with mouldings of English ash from the nearby Bretton Hall estate. It was surmounted on either side by the Huddersfield coat of arms and a red cross on white background. The wheels were fitted with patent puncture-proof double arch India-rubber tyres, and the carriage 'ventilated by Venetian ventilators' over each of the windows, through which curious onlookers could not peer. It was to be pulled by either one or two horses wearing harness also paid for by the funds raised – the harness being furnished with solid nickel and surmounted with a red cross.

It was lit from the outside so offensive fumes from the burning oil would not interfere with the sufferer's comfort, and inside contained everything a qualified medical man would require to deal with accidents of any description.

Its provision meant accident victims could be conveyed to the Infirmary quickly and with much reduced suffering, and without the trying ordeal of being carried, or slowly and laboriously wheeled on a stretcher through the streets, followed perhaps by a crowd, and the focus of hundreds of curious eyes.

Police bands and choirs were often involved in fundraising concerts, and performed regularly in parks and other public spaces to entertain the masses. The opportunity to reveal a more human side to the perceived gruff character of the police helped strengthen relationships between police and populace.

However, one might wonder at the proficiency of Sheffield's police band in 1866 when Alderman Saunders asked if there was any objection to them playing in certain places in the town for the amusement of the public, as was the habit of police bands in other towns. The question was met with laughter – and never answered.

A proliferation of police sports days gave men chance to pitch their athleticism against each other, for prize money. An account from the *Leeds Times*, 21 July 1877, shows the scope of 'athletic sports' in which the police and firemen competed included a sack race, three-legged race, tug-of-war, blind-folded wheelbarrow race, 1-mile walking race, and a race for fat men. The latter was won by Fireman Jowett, with portly PC Thomas Bottomley coming second and receiving 5 shillings for his exertions (£28). All did ample justice to the well-earned dinner provided afterwards in Ilkley.

Chapter 12

Postscript

As both the nineteenth century and Queen Victoria's long reign came to their conclusions, it is interesting to review how policing had progressed over the previous sixty-four years.

From a disjointed miscellany of policing methods in the early part of the century, there were now almost 45,000 men to police the population of over 32.5 million in England and Wales – around one policeman for every 724 people. The aim of complete uniformity of a national police force had still not been achieved, but some constabularies had merged, reducing the number of police forces from 230 to 179.

Pay scales still varied widely. A rookie policeman in Wiltshire was paid only 18 shillings (£100), the same weekly wage as a Leicester constable in 1836. Even Wiltshire men with twenty-five years of service only earned 23s 8d (£131), compared with Leicester's 34 shillings (£189). With final salary pension schemes in place this disparity also had huge impact on retirement income.

Crime statistics from the Home Office show there were 79,516 recorded crimes in 1900, of which around eighty-six percent were thefts and burglaries, 4.5% involved violence against the person, two percent were sexual offences, and the remaining 7.5% 'others' included criminal damage and fraud. The 312 recorded homicides (including infanticide), represented 1 in 104,250 population.

Of the 17,480 people in gaol at the time of the 1901 census, 14,636 were men and 2,844 women.

Developments in technology and equipment had improved policing. The use of photography in the 1860s assisted in recording criminals and identifying repeat offenders.

As early as 1865, Birkenhead's head constable recommended to the watch committee that:

> *Photographic apparatus should be obtained for the use of the police to enable them to detect offenders, by transmitting portraits of prisoners who may be unknown to the Borough Police to various parts of the Kingdom.*[44]

Sharing information thus gathered with colleagues in other parts of the country made apprehension of the right person more straightforward, and by the end of Victoria's reign the possibility of identifying criminals by their fingerprints was also under discussion, the Metropolitan Police establishing its fingerprint branch in July 1901.

Although telegraph technology was first used in apprehending a criminal in 1845, it seems to have taken a further twenty-five years for it to be widely adopted, once continuous refinements made it easier to handle. The cost of installing just one connection between two stations was cited as around £150 (£16,650). Maintenance of Bradford's system was £119 in 1891 (£13,200).

The telegraph was fairly quickly superseded by the telephone. The chief constable in Birkenhead had campaigned to have telephones installed for several years before his wish was granted and all stations were connected in 1887.

Other forces followed suit, with most adopting the technology in the 1890s. Bradford appears to have been a little later as a record in the disciplinary book tells of PC Arthur Lee neglecting to take a telegraph message from the town hall, while at Great Horton Police Station between 2.10pm and 2.30pm on 26 January 1894. PC Mattocks had wired several times without a reply, but unfortunately PC Lee had gone out of the office and 'into the closet' without leaving word.

Bradford certainly had telephones by 1899, as in May it was announced the force was to adopt an extensive system of police telephones in the street, improving communication between officers on the beat and those in stations.

In terms of transport, the horse had been widely in use for decades in some forces, both ridden and used to pull carts and conveyances. Mounted police were invaluable for crowd-control, and, as a means for covering large swathes of countryside, the horse was indispensable to the early superintendents of parochial constables.

However, the bicycle as an efficient means of police transport did not find favour until the 1890s. Forces initially purchased them one at a time. Evidently periods of training were required for constables to achieve the necessary skills to use them successfully, as Cheshire Constabulary kept one at the headquarters specifically for training purposes.

Surrey Police must have acquired good cycling skills as it was reported in January 1896 that they were to purchase a further fourteen bicycles, since the machines had proved very useful in apprehending other cyclists guilty of furious riding and riding without lights – known as 'scorchers'.

In June the same year, by capturing a burglar, the Worcestershire Police demonstrated the advantages of the use of bicycles by the police for running down thieves and others 'wanted'. When information reached Cheltenham and Winchcombe that a man had broken into a cottage at Cleeve, two policemen set out in pursuit on bicycles and overtook the suspect at Tewkesbury, still with the robbery proceeds in his possession.

And finally, as an example of technology, transport and collaboration with neighbouring forces – unimaginable in policing's early days – the *Ipswich Journal* of 5 September 1896 reported on the capture of a defendant:

POSTSCRIPT

It appears that the prisoner did not give himself in charge at the police station, but owing to the smartness of Inspector Summons of the Ipswich Borough Police, he was caught. Harris absconded, and getting a clue, Inspector Summons set off at 5 o'clock on the police bicycle in the direction of Witham. Enquiries led him to Chelmsford, which town he reached at 7 o'clock, a decent two hours' run. From here the officer communicated a description of the man by telephone to the Essex Constabulary at Ingatestone, with the result that Harris was taken and brought straight back.

Notes

1. James, R W. *To the best of our Skill and Knowledge; A Short History of the Cheshire Constabulary 1857 – 1957*
2. ibid
3. Bradford Police Museum exhibit
4. Thompson, Samuel P. (1958) *Maintaining the Queen's Peace, A Short History of the Birkenhead Borough Police*
5. Manchester Libraries, Information and Archives. *Manchester Borough Watch Committee Minutes* 1838-1846 (July 1842)
6. West Yorkshire Archive Service, *Bradford Constable's Disciplinary Report Book*
7. ibid
8. ibid
9. ibid
10. ibid
11. West Yorkshire Archive Service, *Bradford Borough Watch Committee Minutes 1847-1900* (December 1847)
12. Bartlett, Rob. *Surrey Constabulary History*
13. Manchester Libraries, Information and Archives. *Manchester Borough Watch Committee Minutes* 1838-1846 (January 1845)
14. Bartlett, Rob. *Surrey Constabulary History*
15. Manchester Libraries, Information and Archives. *Manchester Borough Watch Committee Minutes* 1838-1846 (July 1846)
16. ibid
17. West Yorkshire Archive Service, *Bradford Borough Watch Committee Minutes 1847-1900* (December 1847)
18. Manchester Libraries, Information and Archives. *Manchester Borough Watch Committee Minutes* 1838-1846 (July 1846)
19. ibid (May 1844)
20. West Yorkshire Archive Service, *Bradford Borough Watch Committee Minutes 1847-1900* (December 1847)
21. Thompson, Samuel P. (1958) *Maintaining the Queen's Peace, A Short History of the Birkenhead Borough Police*

22. West Yorkshire Archive Service, *Bradford Borough Watch Committee Minutes 1847-1900* (December 1847 Instructions to constables)
23. ibid
24. ibid
25. ibid
26. ibid
27. Bartlett, Rob. *Surrey Constabulary History* (Instructions for the guidance of Surrey Constabulary)
28. ibid
29. ibid
30. Thompson, Samuel P. (1958) *Maintaining the Queen's Peace, A Short History of the Birkenhead Borough Police*
31. West Yorkshire Archive Service *West Riding Constabulary Examination Books 1856-1900*
32. The National Archives of the UK, Series HO 26 and HO 27. *England & Wales, Criminal Registers, 1791-1892*
33. West Yorkshire Archive Service, *Bradford Borough Watch Committee Minutes 1847-1900* (June 1848)
34. Cowley, R. & Todd, P. (2006). *The History of Her Majesty's Inspectorate of Constabulary. The first 150 years*
35. West Yorkshire Archive Service, *Bradford Borough Watch Committee Minutes 1847-1900* (June 1860)
36. ibid (July 1860)
37. Manchester Libraries, Information and Archives. *Manchester Borough Watch Committee Minutes* 1838-1846 (February 1845)
38. ibid (April 1845)
39. Thompson, Samuel P. (1958) *Maintaining the Queen's Peace, A Short History of the Birkenhead Borough Police*
40. Greater Manchester Police Museum, *Robert Peacock's Lectures Powers and Responsibilities of the Police (1899)*
42. ibid
43. ibid
44. Thompson, Samuel P. (1958) *Maintaining the Queen's Peace, A Short History of the Birkenhead Borough Police*

Appendices

1) Sir Robert Peel's Nine Principles of Law Enforcement, 1829

1. The basic mission for which police exist is to prevent crime and disorder as an alternative to the repression of crime and disorder by military force and severity of legal punishment.

2. The ability of the police to perform their duties is dependent upon public approval of police existence, actions, behaviour and the ability of the police to secure and maintain public respect.

3. The police must secure the willing co-operation of the public in voluntary observance of the law to be able to secure and maintain public respect.

4. The degree of co-operation of the public that can be secured diminishes, proportionately, to the necessity for the use of physical force and compulsion in achieving police objectives.

5. The police seek and preserve public favour, not by catering to public opinion, but by constantly demonstrating absolutely impartial service to the law, in complete independence of policy, and without regard to the justice or injustice of the substance of individual laws; by ready offering of individual service and friendship to all members of society without regard to their race or social standing, by ready exercise of courtesy and friendly good humour; and by ready offering of individual sacrifice in protecting and preserving life.

6. The police should use physical force to the extent necessary to secure observance of the law or to restore order only when the exercise of persuasion, advice and warning is found to be insufficient to achieve police objectives; and police should use only the minimum degree of physical force which is necessary on any particular occasion for achieving a police objective.

7. The police at all times should maintain a relationship with the public that gives reality to the historic tradition that the police are the public and the public are the police; the police are the only members of the public who are paid to give full-time attention to duties which are incumbent on every citizen in the intent of the community welfare.

8. The police should always direct their actions toward their functions and never appear to usurp the powers of the judiciary by avenging individuals or the state, or authoritatively judging guilt or punishing the guilty.

9. The test of police efficiency is the absence of crime and disorder, not the visible evidence of police action in dealing with them.

2) The Riot Act

PROCLAMATION
Our Sovereign Lady the Queen
Chargeth and commandeth all people being assembled to immediately disperse themselves and peaceably to depart to their habitations, or to their lawful businesses, upon pains contained in the Act made in the 27th year of King George the Third, to prevent tumultuous risings and assemblies.
GOD SAVE THE QUEEN

3) Offences Against the Person Act 1861 s38
'Whosoever shall assault any Person with Intent to commit Felony, or shall assault, resist, or wilfully obstruct any Peace Officer in the due Execution of his Duty, or any Person acting in aid of such Officer, or shall assault any Person with Intent to resist or prevent the lawful Apprehension or Detainer of himself or of any other Person for any Offence, shall be guilty of a Misdemeanour, and being convicted thereof shall be liable, at the Discretion of the Court, to be imprisoned for any Term not exceeding Two Years, with or without Hard Labour.'

Bibliography

Noel E. Smith: *Helmets, Handcuffs and Hoses, The Story of the Wallasey Police and Fire Brigade Part One* ISBN- 0-9517762-3-1

Peter Wroe: *A History of Policing in Warrington*

History of Derbyshire Constabulary

Richard Cowley, Peter Todd, Louise Ledger: *The History of Her Majesty's Inspectorate of Constabulary the first 150 years (2006)*

Longenden Amenity Society 1974: *Reminiscences of a Chief Constable: William Chadwick, Chief Constable of Stalybridge.*

Bryn Elliott: *Peelers Progress. Policing Waltham Abbey since 1840* (2001)

Sergeant Samuel P. Thompson: *Maintaining the Queen's Peace, A Short History of the Birkenhead Borough Police* (1958)

Museum of Policing in Cheshire: *A Short History of the Macclesfield Borough Police Force from its inception in 1836 to amalgamation with the Cheshire Constabulary in 1974* (Compilation)

Clifford R. Stanley, Leicester Archaeological and History Society 1976: *A Centenary Tribute to Frederick Goodyer*

A History of Policing in Lancashire

To the Best of our Skill and Knowledge; A Short History of the Cheshire Constabulary 1857 – 1957: Compiled by R. W. James, former chief constable of Congleton and later superintendent of Cheshire Constabulary, Museum of Policing in Cheshire

Joe Heller, Liverpool City Police: *Policing in 19th Century Liverpool*

Rob Bartlett: *Surrey Constabulary History*

Gordon Smith: *History of Bradford City Police* (1974) ISBN 1-095036-83-0X

Philip Rawlings: *Policing: A Short History* (2002) Willan Publishing ISBN 1-903240-27-1

Resources

Bradford Borough Watch Committee Minutes 1847-1900 (West
  Yorkshire Archive Service)
Manchester Borough Watch Committee Minutes 1838-1846
  (Courtesy of Gerard Lodge, Manchester Family History Research)
Salford Watch Committee minutes 1844 (Greater Manchester Police
  Museum Archives)
Bradford Constable's Defaulters Book 1870-1898 (West Yorkshire
  Archive Service)
Bradford Constable's Disciplinary Report Book (West Yorkshire
  Archive Service)
West Riding Constabulary Examination Books 1856-1900 (West
  Yorkshire Archive Service)
Leeds Police Register of Constables 1833-1914 (West Yorkshire
  Archive Service)
Bradford Police Museum
Greater Manchester Police Museum
Kent Police Museum
Cambridgeshire Police Museum
The British Newspaper Archive
HISTPOP.ORG (Online Historical Population Reports)
Victorian Crime & Punishment: http://vcp.e2bn.org
Victorian Police Stations: http://www.victorianpolicestations.org
British Police History: http://british-police-history.uk
The Police History Society: http://www.policehistorysociety.co.uk
The Museum of Policing in Cheshire:
  http://www.museumofpolicingincheshire.org.uk
Home Office: Official Statistics Historical Crime Data
House of Commons Parliamentary Papers; The Select Committee on
  Police 1853
Licensing Act 1872: The National Archives via
  http://www.legislation.gov.uk
A Web of English History: http://www.historyhome.co.uk

Index

INDEX

Livery Stable Company, 136
Observer, newspaper, 7, 32, 126, 129
prison van, 99
Brannagan, PC Thomas, 42–3
Broadmoor Lunatic Asylum, 118
Bromley:
  Bromley and District Times,
    newspaper, 166
  police force, 166

C
Caistor, 29
Cambridgeshire, 28
Cartwright, Major General William,
  149, 152
Castleford,108
Chartism, 119
Chartists, 23, 57–8, 119–23
  see also Tyler, Wat; Sagar, William;
    Wilsden
Cheetham:
  township, 18
Chelmsford, 173
Cheshire, 4–5, 110–11, 130
  Constabulary, 31, 98, 160, 172
Chester, 4, 22
Chidswell colliery, 134
Chorlton upon Medlock:
  township, 18
Christopher Sykes MP, 135
City of Bath:
  police force, 29, 156
City of London:
  police force, 30, 60–1, 63, 142
Class of Merit (Merit Class), 41–3, 80
Clough Head, Golcar, Huddersfield,
  112
Cobbe, Colonel, 44, 106
Colbeck, Ruth, 114–5
  see also Assaults on police,
    Winpenny, Police Sergeant

Cork Examiner, newspaper, 127–8
County and Borough Police Act:
  1856, 30, 149,
  1859, 153
County Police Act:
  1839, 23, 150,
  1840, 152
Crow, Police Inspector, 117

D
Deasey, Captain, 124–5
  see also Fenians
Derby Gaol, 99
Derbyshire, 110
Despard, Chief Constable Captain,
  West Riding Constabulary, 134
Dewsbury, 114, 137
Disorderly women, 75
Doncaster, 106
  sessions, 43–4
  races, 132, 135
Dover, 17
Dublin:
  Daily Express, newspaper, 133
  police force, 38, 60–1, 63, 65, 124,
    142
  Warder and Dublin Mail, newspaper,
    57
Duke of Wellington, 11
Duke of Westminster, 69
Dukinfield, 130

E
Essex, 28
  Constabulary, 173

F
Featherstone, 132
felonies, 2, 43, 89–93
Fenians, 38, 123–7, 130
  see also Allen; Deasey; Gould; Larkin

181

INDEX

183

INDEX

Portsmouth, 17

Poyser, PC Herbert, 109

Prevention of Crimes Act 1871, 88

Prison vans, 98–102, 124

Prize fights, 109–10

Punishment by Death Act 1832, 103

R

Reform Act 1832, 10

Reform Bill 1867, 127

Riot Act, 122, 128, 132, 134, 177

Riotous or disorderly behaviour, 67, 70–3, 94

Ripon, 126

Roberts, Thomas, 74–5

Robinson, Sgt Major William, 61

Rochdale, 3, 136

Rowan, Colonel Sir Charles, Metropolitan Police, 12, 22

Rural Constabularies Act 1839 (aka County Police Act/ Rural Police Act), 23

Rural Police Act 1839 (aka County Police Act/Rural Constabularies Act), 23

Russell, Captain, Chief Constable, West Riding Constabulary, 45

S

Salford:
   Borough Police Force, 25–6

Salt, Titus, 137

Saltersbrook, near Woodhead, 110
   see also Prize fights

Select Committees:
   1852 To consider the expediency of adopting a more uniform system of police in England, Scotland and Wales, 28–30
   1875 To inquire into the Police Superannuation Funds in the

Counties and Boroughs of England and Wales, 156–8
   1877 To look at the problems of intemperance, 68–9, 71, 139

Shaw, Sir Charles, Chief Commissioner, Manchester, 19–22

Sheffield, 44, 46–7, 85–6, 110, 133,
   Daily Telegraph, newspaper, 85
   Independent, newspaper, 43, 45

Shrewsbury, 127
   see also Fenians

Somerset:
   Constabulary, 156
   see also Superannuation

Southampton:
   police force, 17, 166–7

South Wales Daily News, newspaper, 134

Special High Constable, Cheshire, 5–6,

Staffordshire, 80, 108, 130

Statute of Winchester 1285, 1

Stephens, James, 123–4
   see also Fenians

Stockport:
   Borough Police Force, 151

Strangeways Gaol, 99

Superannuation:
   police relief fund, 154–5
   superannuation fund, 105, 148, 152–8

Supernumeraries, 26, 33, 36, 40

Surfleet, Police Constable, 87

Surrey:
   Constabulary, 33, 39, 44, 69, 91, 139, 172

Sykes, Superintendent George, West Riding Constabulary 45–7

T

Taylor, William, 115–8

185